THE CREST AND THE HIDE

THE CREST
AND
THE HIDE

AND OTHER AFRICAN STORIES
OF HEROES, CHIEFS, BARDS,
HUNTERS, SORCERERS AND
COMMON PEOPLE

◆ ◆ ◆

HAROLD COURLANDER

ILLUSTRATIONS BY
MONICA VACHULA

COWARD, MC CANN & GEOGHEGAN, INC.

NEW YORK

Text copyright © 1982 by Harold Courlander
Illustrations copyright © 1982 by Monica Vachula
"The First Bard Among the Soninke," "Kirama and Kankejan"
and "The Great Snake of Wagadou" first appeared in
African Arts magazine.
Designed by Mike Suh
First printing
Printed in the United States of America

Library of Congress Cataloging in Publication Data
Main entry under title:
The Crest and the hide.
Contents: The first bard among the Soninke (Soninke,
Mali)—A chief names his heirs (Ashanti, Ghana)—The
crest and the hide (Lega, Zaire)—[etc.]
1. Tales, African. [1. Folklore—Africa]
I. Courlander, Harold, date. II. Vachula, Monica, ill.
PZ8.1.C874 398.2'096 81-9739
ISBN 0-698-20536-7 AACR2

CONTENTS

THE
FIRST BARD AMONG
THE SONINKE

♦ *Soninke* ♦

In ancient times there were two brothers who went hunting for game in the bush. They traveled far, but they did not find any game to kill. One, two, three days they were in the bush, hunting, hunting. They did not find anything. They became lost. They did not know how to return to their village. Hunger overtook them. Because it was the dry season, there was no fruit for them to eat. Because they could not find game, they had no meat to eat.

On the fourth day the younger brother said to the older: "My brother, I cannot go any farther. I am too hungry. I have no strength to go on. If I am to die, I will die here."

The older brother answered: "Yes, rest here. You are my younger brother and I do not want you to die. I will go on ahead and try to find a small animal of some kind. Then you will have something to eat. Wait for me. I will come back."

The older brother left the younger and went ahead. He did not find anything. There was no game of any kind. At last he took out his knife and cut a piece of meat from his thigh, and after that he returned to where his younger brother was waiting. He said: "Oh yes! I found a small animal and killed it. I will make a fire. I will cook the meat for you. When you have eaten it, you will feel strong again." He made a fire and cooked the meat. When it was ready, he gave it to the younger brother. The younger brother ate, and his strength returned.

After a while the older brother saw smoke in the distance and knew there must be a village out there. He said: "Oh younger brother, don't you see the smoke in the distance? There is a village at that place. Now we will be saved from starvation. I will go ahead to make certain, then I will come back for you."

The younger brother answered: "No, now I feel strong again. I will go with you."

So they started out. They traveled toward the place where the smoke was rising. The older brother kept his bloody thigh covered as best he could, but blood stained his clothing. When the younger brother saw that, he asked: "What is it? What happened to you?" He uncovered the older brother's wound. He touched it. Then he understood everything.

He said: "Yes, my older brother! Now I understand what you have done for me. You saved my life with flesh taken from your thigh. To give someone your own flesh and blood is the greatest expression of love. Henceforth I will be your dieli—the bard who sings of your great deeds and of the history of your family. Whatever you ask of me, I will do it. I will follow you and serve you. My family will follow your family. My grandson will follow your grandson. My descendants will follow your descendants forever. We will be as slaves to your people until the end of time and sing praises of your noble character."

The younger brother became the slave and bard of the older brother. His descendants became slaves and bards of the older brother's descendants. They were called dieli, meaning blood, because of the older brother's blood gift that had saved the younger brother's life. Because they wished to please their masters, the dieli became accomplished singers and musicians, and they sang stories of times that had passed, of great events and ancestor heroes. To this day the bards pass their knowledge and their songs on to their sons, and the sons become the bards and historians of the family descended from the older brother.

Of the two brothers who went hunting together in the bush, the younger brother became the first dieli, and ever since that day it has been the custom for noble families to have bards to recall the happenings of ancient days.

A CHIEF NAMES
HIS HEIRS

♦ *Ashanti* ♦

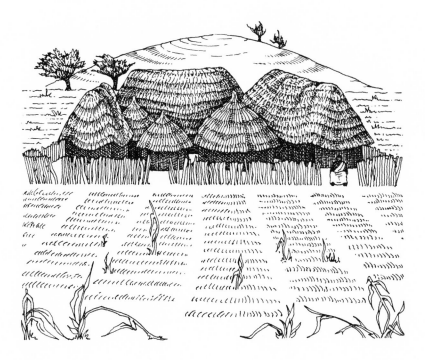

There was a chief living in Dagomba. He was growing old, and he began to think of how his estate would be disposed of when he died. Now, according to the traditions of those times, a man's estate was given not to his son but to his sister's son; that is to say, to his nephew. The chief had much wealth—large fields, granaries stocked with corn, and many servants and slaves. He wondered if his nephew would be able to take care of this estate wisely. He said to himself: "How do I know that my nephew will not let the fields go uncared for, abuse my slaves, and squander everything away?"

One day when he felt that his life was growing short, the chief sent for his nephew and said to him: "My nephew, you are the one who is supposed to inherit from me. I want you to inherit thoughtfully. Therefore, when I am dead and my property is disposed of, you will select one thing that I own and claim it for yourself. Everything else I will leave to my head slave, for he has been loyal and faithful to me all his life. I speak of it now so that you will have time to decide what you value most."

The nephew went away, thinking, "What moves my uncle to behave this way? Am I not his nephew? He tells me, 'Inherit thoughtfully. Take only one thing.' Shall I take his gun, or his garden, or the tree in his courtyard and leave everything else of value to his head slave?" The nephew was troubled. He thought: "Why should I even attend the gathering where the legacy will be made public? No, he rejects me. Therefore I want nothing from him at all."

But the young man could not get the matter out of his mind. He did not eat, he did not sleep. He told his mother: "My uncle puts me aside. He says, 'Take one thing from my estate. The rest I will give to my head slave.'" His mother answered: "Perhaps there is a meaning in it that you do not understand. He may be testing you." The young man thought about it, but he could not find an answer.

The chief died. They buried him and held a funeral feast. The time came when the chief's spokesman was to reveal how the estate would be distributed. People of the town gathered in front of the chief's house. The nephew also came, for in the night as he slept an answer had appeared in his dream.

The chief's spokesman announced to the crowd that the nephew was to select one thing, and that all the rest would go to the head slave. When the people heard that, they resented it. They said: "It is unjust. When before this has a man denied his nephew a rightful inheritance?"

The nephew spoke, saying, "I have pondered this matter deeply. I thought perhaps I would not come, or that I would say, 'Give everything to the slave, because he has been a faithful servant to my uncle.' But my uncle said to me, 'Inherit thoughtfully.' He wanted to be certain that I would not waste his fields and granaries by neglect. I shall do as he advised. Therefore I choose one thing—my uncle's head slave."

The chief's spokesman said to the people: "You are witnesses. The nephew chooses the head slave. The head slave receives everything else." And the crowd called out: "We are witnesses!"

The spokesman said: "It has been witnessed. Though the nephew inherits one man as his share, yet he inherits everything, because the property of a slave is likewise the property of his master. What a slave owns, the master owns. You, nephew of the chief, you have inherited thoughtfully, as the chief desired. This is what we say to you:

Do not waste what has been given to you.
Never say, "With my own effort I created this estate."
Do not abuse your laborers, because they put food in your mouth.
When a sickle breaks, we put a new blade in it.
You are the new blade. May your fields flourish.
As you have inherited thoughtfully, live thoughtfully.

And the nephew answered:

"Sir, I accept my inheritance gratefully and with humility. My uncle's head slave was led to believe he would inherit wealth, and now he finds he has nothing. Will anyone accuse me of wasting my estate if I give this man a field, a house, and a granary of his own?"

The chief's spokesman said: "No, they will praise you for an honorable deed."

So the chief's bequest was settled, and his words to his nephew became a saying:

"Inherit thoughtfully."

THE CREST
AND THE HIDE

◆ *Lega* ◆

There were two friends. One went to the house of the other and said: "Because you are my friend, I am coming to you to ask for help. There was a young woman I wanted for my wife. I went to her house to plead for her, but in the night she had died. The father said to me, 'My daughter has gone to the Land of the Dead.' This young woman, I want her very much. Therefore, my friend, I ask you to go to that place, the Land of the Dead, to find her and bring her back."

His friend replied: "That is a big thing. To enter the ground and find the trail to the place of the dead is difficult. What trail shall I take? What dangerous creatures will block my way? And when I arrive and say I want to bring the young woman back, will they let me do it? No, they will attack me. Perhaps they will kill me. I will remain forever in that country and you will not see me any more. I will become another one of the dead who remain there and cannot return."

The first man said: "Yes, it is a big thing that has to be done. You are the only person I can ask to do it."

The second man said: "Let me speak of my little sister. Years ago she went with her water jar to the river. A spirit in the form of a water snake appeared. He came out of the water. He took my sister and descended into the river. My parents grieved. I want my sister back. Therefore, you, my friend, make a journey for me. Go down into the river and find her. I have asked others to make this search, but they all replied, 'Am I

15

your closest friend that I should be asked?' What they said was true. You are my closest friend. Therefore I am asking you to make the journey."

The first friend answered: "If I should go on such a journey would I ever return? Who knows what lies at the bottom of the river? It is dark down there. Surely there are monsters guarding the place. Who has ever gone to the city of the water snake and come back alive?"

The second friend said: "Yes, as you see, it is a brave deed that has to be done."

The first friend said: "Very well. You enter the earth first and go to the Land of the Dead to find my young woman. When you return, I will go down into the river to find your sister."

The second friend answered: "No, first you search for my sister, then I will look for your young woman."

The first said: "If I should die while searching in the river for your sister, why, I would never see my young woman when you bring her back."

The two friends argued. They could not agree. At last they went to an old man of the village to judge their dispute. They told him what each of them wanted the other to do. He listened. He considered the matter. Then he said:

"I have heard everything. Now, my sons, listen carefully while I speak of two other friends, water lizard and guinea fowl. They were close. Whatever one owned he shared with the other. In the village where they lived, each creature took his turn as chief, first one and then another. A time came when the people went to water lizard and said, 'You, water lizard, it is your turn. Prepare yourself for the chief-making ceremony.'

"The water lizard prepared himself. He wanted everything to be elaborate. He wanted to look splendid. He wanted everyone to know that he was worthy of being chief. He acquired the things he needed for the chief-making ceremony. He had the drum, the hide on which he would sit, his ceremonial clothes, and beer to give out to all those who came. He lacked only one thing, the feathers for his headdress.

"So he sent his slave to the guinea fowl for help. The slave said to the guinea fowl: 'My master asks you for a crest of feathers for his headdress.' The guinea fowl collected the crests of birds and fowls and sent them to the water lizard. But the water lizard rejected them. He sent his slave again to the guinea fowl. The slave said: 'My master says that none of the crests is splendid enough for the ceremony. He wants the crest from your own head.' The guinea fowl was unhappy. But at last, because he was the water lizard's friend, he took the beautiful feathers from his head and sent them in the care of the slave. Now the water lizard had everything he wanted for the chief-making ceremony. But from that day on, the guinea fowl's head was naked.

"Time passed, and one day the people came to the guinea fowl, saying, 'Prepare yourself. It is your turn to become chief.' The guinea fowl prepared. He acquired a drum. His wife swept the courtyard of his house. He prepared beer for all who would attend the ceremony. He lacked only one thing—a good hide to sit upon. He sent his slave to the water lizard with the message, 'My master needs a beautiful hide for the ceremony.' The water lizard hunted, and he sent all kinds of hides to the guinea fowl. But the guinea fowl said: 'No, they will not do. Only one hide will be beautiful enough, the one you are wearing.' The water lizard did not want to part with his hide. He asked his wife what he should do. She said: 'He is your friend. What you asked of him, he gave it. What he asks for, you must give it to him.' So the water lizard removed his hide and sent it to the guinea fowl. After that he died."

The old man who was judging the dispute said: "You young men who are friends, the guinea fowl and the water lizard also were friends. Each of them asked for something great. First, one asked; then, the other asked. In the end the guinea fowl became bald and the water lizard lost his hide and found death. One asked for something too great, and the other responded by asking for something still greater. Each of them went beyond friendship. That should not be the way between friends. If you ask a friend for something, ask only what is reasonable. If you ask too much, he will ask you too much. Thus we have the saying:

"'Do not ask a friend for more than he can give.' And we also say, 'If you ask for a crest, you may have to pay with a hide.'"

The two young men went away. They spoke no more about their dispute. They did not go searching under the river or in the Land of the Dead.

THE CHIEF OF AGOGO AND THE CHIEF OF MAMPO

♦ *Ashanti* ♦

There was a chief in the town of Agogo. His name was Nana Adu. One night he was in his house drinking palm wine. He began speaking loudly. Although he was alone, he was addressing his remarks to Nana Kofi, the chief of the neighboring town of Mampo. The sound of his voice grew louder and was heard outside.

A man named Dako was passing, and hearing Nana Adu's voice, he stopped to listen. He heard Nana Adu say:

"You, Nana Kofi, who sit on a stool and hold court under your great fig tree, how do you govern your town? When the enemy comes, do you summon your young men to follow you into battle, or do you go inside your house and close your door? When there is famine in the land, do you share with the people whatever you have in your granary, or do you hide your corn and keep it for yourself? You, Nana Kofi of Mampo, how is it with you when the wells dry up? Do you invite the people to take water from your own private spring, or do you tell them to go elsewhere? If another man's cow strays into your field, do you tell your slave to take it back to its rightful owner? Or do you say, 'Kill the cow and prepare a feast for my household'? And when two men come to you with a complaint, do you listen to both and ponder justice? Or do you say, 'The first man, I like him; the second man, I do not like him. Therefore I will judge in favor of the first man'? And when your slaves are old and tired, do you tell them, 'Live on in your house as always. I will feed you'? Or do you turn them out to fend for themselves?"

Standing near Nana Adu's house, Dako heard these words. He said to himself: "I thought Nana Adu and Nana Kofi were friends. Now I know what our chief has never said in public, that Nana Kofi is his enemy. If Kofi is Adu's enemy, he is our town's enemy also. Yes, now I know everything."

One day when Dako was on the road between the two towns he saw a man coming. It was the son-in-law of Nana Kofi of Mampo. When the man approached, Dako said to him: "I know you. You are the son-in-law of Nana Kofi, who hides in his house when the enemy is near. Son-in-law of Nana Kofi, who keeps all his corn to himself when famine comes. Son-in-law of Nana Kofi, who takes other people's cows and slaughters them for himself. Son-in-law of Nana Kofi, who does not know the meaning of justice. Son-in-law of Nana Kofi, who turns his old slaves into the bush to fend for themselves."

Nana Kofi's son-in-law was astonished to hear himself accosted this way, but he did not reply. He went on to the town of Agogo. He went to the chief's house and spoke to him, reporting how he had been insulted on the road. Nana Adu sent for Dako. He said: "Why did you insult my friend, the chief of Mampo, and abuse his son-in-law on the road?"

Dako answered: "Why, I only said this and that, the words I heard you speaking loudly one night in your house. The chief of Mampo surely must be your enemy. It was only for this reason that I spoke as I did to his son-in-law."

Nana Adu said: "Man, you are a fool. When you heard me speaking like that I was asking questions of myself. You heard the questions, but you did not listen to the answers. I was measuring my own conduct to see whether or not I always behave honorably, for a chief sometimes forgets his responsibilities. My friend, Nana Kofi, is respected for fulfilling all his obligations as a chief. Often at night I ask myself if I am following Nana Kofi's good example. So I say, 'You, Kofi of Mampo, do you run away from battle?' And I say in reply, speaking quietly, 'No, you do not hide from battle. I will follow your example. I will be courageous.' Then I say, 'You, Kofi of Mampo, do you mistreat your slaves?' And I answer in a quiet voice. 'No, you treat your faithful slaves with affection. I will follow your example and do the same.' I ask, 'You, Nana Kofi, do you give justice to the man you like and injustice to the man you do not like?' And I answer quietly, perhaps without letting a sound come from my mouth, 'No, justice has nothing to do with liking or disliking.' In this manner I frequently address Nana Kofi of Mampo because of his good character, always measuring my conduct alongside his. You, Dako, you heard only the questions, and you did not want to know any more. You appointed yourself the translator and spokesman for the chief."

Dako was silent. He could think of nothing to say in his own defense. Nana Adu said: "The words you spoke on the road were your own. They insulted my friend Nana Kofi and his son-in-law who has never done us any harm. For these insults you will pay Nana Kofi's son-in-law two cows in damages. Do not lurk any more outside the chief's house at night listening to what you do not understand. And when your ears drink in another person's words, keep your lips closed tightly so that the words do not drip off your tongue. A man's head should be like a strong box to contain things, not like a sieve to scatter words wherever he goes. I quote you the proverb of Anansi.

"Anansi, the spider, says: 'If you know the questions but not the answers, you do not know half of everything. You know nothing at all.'"

THE
WONDERFUL THING

♦ *Bemba* ♦

In a certain village, the chief sent his messenger on an errand to a neighboring town. Returning from the town, the messenger followed a trail through the bush, and he came upon an enormous snake sunning itself among the rocks. He said: "Hu! Who has ever seen so large a snake before now?" He did not approach the creature for fear of being eaten, but he sang a song to soothe it so that he could pass safely. He sang:

> *You who lie there in the sun,*
> *You are a wonderful thing!*
> *Surely you have made men run away,*
> *You are a wonderful thing!*
> *Where else in the world is a snake like you?*
> *You are a wonderful thing!*

The snake was soothed by the song, and the messenger passed along the trail. The messenger went directly to his chief and said: "I went to the town, and on my way home through the bush I saw a wonderful thing. I discovered a huge snake, larger than any other seen by men. It is thick as a tree, and were it stretched out to its full length it would reach from your house to the river. He has a beautiful color, too, and when a person sings to him he listens."

The chief said: "The snake you describe is truly a wonderful thing. It is something I would like to have in my village.

Therefore bring it to me." The messenger said: "O chief, he is far too large for me to carry. He would swallow me at once." The chief said impatiently: "Well, in that case let the whole village go." The messenger replied: "O chief, where will we put him when we have brought him here?" The chief said: "Let a special house be built in the village." So the men of the village gathered and constructed a new house, and the women brought bundles of grass to cover the roof. They stamped the floor of the house with their feet to make it firm, and they swept all around to make the ground clean. When that was done, the chief said: "Do not loiter. Go now to get the wonderful thing."

All the people of the village went into the bush to the place where the enormous snake was living. They saw that it was the largest snake in the bush. They gathered in a circle and sang to soothe the snake and make it calm. Then they picked it up and carried it over their shoulders in a long line. The village drummer played his drum, signaling that an important visitor had arrived. Carefully, the people placed the great snake in the house they had built for it and closed the door. They stood before the house, singing:

> *You who have come to our village,*
> *You are a wonderful thing!*
> *Where else in the world is a snake like you?*
> *You are a wonderful thing!*

And while they sang, the messenger went to get the chief. The chief came, his elephant-tail switch in his hand.

They opened the door of the house so the chief could see what they had brought. He looked. He flicked his elephant-tail switch. He said: "What is this?" They said: "O chief, it is the wonderful thing we brought for you from the bush." The chief said: "This is nothing but a snake. Do we need such a thing? Take it back where it came from."

KIRAMA AND KANKEJAN

♦ Soninke ♦

There was once a small kingdom called Segou, and in a village of that kingdom lived Kone, an aged woman, and her granddaughter. The people of the village gave Kone jakka; that is to say, they gave her food so that she and the young girl could survive. That was the custom in former days. Those who had food shared with those who did not. A rich family set aside one-twentieth of its crops or sheep to give as jakka to the old, the crippled, and other unfortunate persons. The spirit of jakka was the spirit of respect for all who lived in the village.

For some time, the old woman and her granddaughter received a part of the people's crops and meat. But a day came when the people became careless and forgot them. They no longer provided the woman with anything. Because she was old she could not do all the things necessary to sustain her life in dignity.

So Kone became bitter and pronounced a malediction on the village, saying, "You have forgotten about me. I no longer receive the respect to which I am entitled. Therefore you will share my misfortune. The rains that water your fields will stop falling. Your crops will dry up. As I suffer, you too will suffer." What the old woman Kone said came to pass. The rains stopped falling. The fields dried up and turned brown. The food that people had stored away was eaten, and in order to go on living they turned more and more to hunting game in the bush.

But Kone transformed herself into a ferocious rhinoceros, and when hunters went into the bush to find meat, she killed them.

She had the magic power to do this. The rhinoceros was an extension of herself. She did not disappear from her house. She remained there as before, but the extension of herself lived in the bush as a rhinoceros, and the rhinoceros made life very difficult for the people. Many hunters went into the bush and never returned. The village agreed that if it was to survive, the rhinoceros had to be destroyed. The best of hunters went into the bush to kill her, but they could not do it. Their bullets would not penetrate her hide.

The people began to go hungry. The chief sent messengers to far-off places asking help from their hunters. In the neighboring kingdom of Manding were two brothers who were skilled in hunting. The elder was Kirama and the younger was Kankejan. They went to their father and told him they wished to go to Segou to kill the ferocious rhinoceros. Their father listened. He said: "Yes, I am willing for you to do this. But first go to the village of Kaba and tell your intentions to Simbo Kalaba. He is a learned man with magical powers."

So the two young men went to Kaba to consult with Simbo Kalaba. They explained to him what they were going to do. He said: "Yes, I understand. Wait a little. Come back after a while and we shall speak of it again." The brothers went away. Simbo Kalaba brought out his divining tray and put sand in it. He moved the sand about with his fingers, and he read its meaning.

When Kirama and Kankejan returned, he spoke to them this way: "The task you are undertaking is difficult. It cannot be accomplished in the ordinary way. You will not defeat this fierce animal by force. You will not win by sorcery. You will

34

not win by courage or heroic deeds. You can win only by respect and consideration." What Simbo Kalaba said to Kirama and Kankejan had meaning within, but what the meaning was they did not understand.

Simbo Kalaba also said: "I read in the sand that you will arrive at a certain village. The people there will give you a girl as a gift. She will be poor, and she may appear ugly. Take her. Bring her to me. In this way you will repay me for divining for you."

The brothers departed. They journeyed. In time they came to the kingdom of Segou. They entered a village, where they saw an old woman carrying a heavy load of firewood on her head. They said: "Grandmother, let us help you. We will carry your firewood." Now, the old woman was Kone. Because of her magical powers, when she saw the two brothers she knew that they had come to kill her—that is to say, the rhinoceros that was an extension of herself. But they did not know who she was. They perceived her only as an old woman carrying firewood. They said again: "It is proper for the young to help the old. Give us the firewood. We will carry it."

Kone answered: "No. I don't want any help. Why should you carry my firewood? I don't need you." The brothers persisted, saying, "You are old, grandmother. It is not right for you to carry when we can carry for you." Kone did not answer. She continued walking. Kirama and Kankejan followed her, repeating that they would carry her wood, but she did not stop. So one of the brothers said: "Grandmother, let us give you some of our milk to take home with you." She answered: "No, I don't want your milk." The other brother said: "Well, then, take these two kola nuts." Kone refused, saying, "Why do you persist? I don't need anything." The brothers followed her to her house, but she went in without accepting the kola nuts.

Kirama and Kankejan went then to the chief of the village. They explained to him that they had come to kill the ferocious rhinoceros. The chief said: "The beast can be killed only by exceptional hunters." The brothers answered: "We are good hunters. That is why we have made the journey from Manding." So the chief had a welcome feast prepared for the brothers, and gave them a house to sleep in. The feast that was prepared was chicken and rice.

Now, whenever an animal was killed it was divided in a certain way. Each part had a special meaning. The head meant something, the breast meant something, the legs meant something. The neck belonged to the person who killed it. So when the chicken was brought to Kirama and Kankejan, they divided it. They took the breast and a leg of the chicken to Kone and offered them to her.

Kone said: "Hé! Why are you bringing me these parts?" The brothers said: "We bring them out of respect." Kone said: "I have heard your names, Kirama and Kankejan. What do I have to do with Kirama and Kankejan? Are we related? No. Yet you bring me the breast, which is reserved for a person's grandmother. I am not your grandmother. You bring me the leg, which is reserved for one's sister. I am not your sister." However, after saying this, Kone accepted the meat, for there was a saying that even if one's enemy offered meat it should be accepted. Having given Kone the breast and the leg, Kirama and Kankejan returned to their house.

36

Every day after that they brought things to the old woman—groundnuts, milk, and other kinds of food. They began to sense that Kone had knowledge and special powers. On the fifth day, Kone came to visit them. They conversed until it was late, and when she was ready to leave they accompanied her home. Before entering her house she said: "Young men, you have given me the respect that the people of the village have forgotten to give. If others had done the same, the village would not now be suffering. Therefore I am going to reveal secret knowledge to you. In saying what I am about to say I am putting myself in your hands. I am ready to do this because I want to die respected, not abandoned and forgotten."

The brothers didn't understand what Kone was saying. She seemed to be speaking in riddles. She went on: "I know that you came here to kill the rhinoceros. I knew it before you even spoke to the chief. I am the one you came to kill, for I am the rhinoceros who roams in the bush. But you respected me even though I am old and poor. I give the secret to you. I brought misery on the village because it forgot the duty and the meaning of respect. Once I was a respected grandmother of the village, and the people brought me jakka so that my granddaughter and I could go on living in dignity. Then we faded from everyone's mind. I am too old now to farm. I am too old to fish. I am no longer regarded as worthwhile, and no one brings me anything. This is why the people are suffering. Just as I have nothing, they have nothing. We are equal again. If the whole village is poor, then I am no different from them."

The old woman went on, saying, "Now, before I tell you the things you have to know, let us go to the edge of the village." It was the custom in those days that when a solemn contract was to be made, it was done outside the village at the edge of the bush where everything was neutral. Kone, Kirama, and Kankejan squatted down, so that they were neither sitting nor standing, suspended between earth and sky, because this was what people did when they made pledges to one another. Kone said: "These are the pledges to be made. I will reveal to you the way in which the rhinoceros can be killed. In return, you will promise me happiness for my granddaughter. When you leave here, take her with you and see that she is treated well. On this condition I give you my life." The brothers answered: "Yes, grandmother, we agree."

The old woman said: "Good. Now, this is what must be done. Follow the south trail from the village. There is a grove of trees, and beyond it another grove. Beyond the second grove is the water hole where I go to drink every morning just as the sun is rising. Be there on time. You will see me coming from the water hole. Do not place bullets in your gun, because bullets cannot harm me. What you should place in the gun is this: two kola nuts, some sheep dung, and rice water." After saying that, the old woman returned to her house in the village.

Kirama and Kankejan also returned to their house. They discussed what the old woman had told them. Kirama, the older brother, said: "How can we believe what Kone told us? To kill a rhinoceros one must have a bullet. The old woman must be mad." Kankejan said: "Older brother, we traveled a great distance with a purpose in mind. We came to accomplish something no other hunters have been able to do. We have already been here one month. Let us do as the old woman says."

So the next morning before dawn they followed the south trail from the village. When they reached the second grove they saw that the water hole was just beyond. They prepared their gun as the old woman had instructed them, placing in it two kola nuts, rice water, and sheep dung. After doing this, they climbed a tree. Kirama still did not believe that the gun could kill anything. But when the rhinoceros came from the water hole, Kankejan shot it. With only one shot he killed the rhinoceros. Kirama did not believe the animal was dead. He did not want to come down from the tree. Kankejan came down. He put his foot on the dead animal, saying, "You see, older brother, it is dead. Come down, come down." Kirama would not come down. He said: "Before I will believe the rhinoceros is dead you will have to cut off its tail and show it to me."

Then the younger brother cut off the animal's tail and held it up for Kirama to see. Kirama saw that the animal was truly dead. He began to sing a praise song about Kankejan: "O my younger brother, you are brave! You have performed a heroic and glorious deed!" He recited Kankejan's ancestry and all the courageous things he had done in his life.

There are some who say that when Kankejan cut off the tail of the rhinoceros it was the beginning of a tradition. Thereafter, whenever a hunter killed an animal in the bush he cut off its tail and displayed it as proof of his accomplishment. It is also said that when Kirama sang the praise song to Kankejan he became the first bard or griot of the Diabate family, which traces its ancestry to Kankejan. Since that day descendants of Kankejan have been praised in poems sung by descendants of Kirama.

The two brothers returned to the village and showed the

people the tail of the dead rhinoceros, saying, "We have killed the fierce animal in the bush. Now you may go safely hunting for meat." The village was happy. Everyone admired Kirama and Kankejan for their accomplishment.

Now, it was the custom in those days that whenever someone performed a worthwhile deed, the chief would reward him with a gift. The chief would ask him what he wanted, and the person would indicate what he wished to have as a prize. So the chief asked the brothers to name their reward. They were thinking now about the debt that they owed to Simbo Kalaba, the wise man who had divined for them. So they answered: "The only thing we want is a young girl for a wife."

The chief said: "Good." He ordered a festival to be held. He instructed that all the village's unmarried girls should be there. The festival began. Many of the girls were beautiful, but the brothers did not choose any of them. They said to the chief: "We do not see the one we are looking for." The chief answered: "The village can offer you only what it has." The brothers answered impatiently: "Ah! Did you bring all of them? Are there no others?"

Then one of the chief's advisors said: "Oh, perhaps there is still one more. An old woman named Kone has just died. She had a granddaughter." Another advisor said: "You speak of the old shabby woman who lived on the outskirts of the village, and the dirty beggar girl who stayed in her house with her? Do not think about it. Heroes would not accept such a present from a chief." The first advisor replied: "Who knows what they are looking for? They have rejected all the others."

So the people brought Kone's granddaughter from her house.

She did not resemble the others in any way. Her skin did not shine. Her clothes were only rags. Poverty had made her ugly. But Kirama and Kankejan said immediately: "Yes, this is the one we like." People of the village turned to one another, saying: "Haah? This is the one? All these beautiful girls and they choose the old woman's granddaughter?"

But the chief saw that the brothers were in earnest. He said: "If she is truly the one you want, take her."

Kirama and Kankejan took the girl. They left the country of Segou and returned to Manding. They brought the girl to Simbo Kalaba, the diviner. They said: "We accomplished what we went to do." Simbo Kalaba said: "Yes, I know. I read it in the sand." They said: "It was as you described it. We did not defeat the rhinoceros through heroism, but through respect. The old woman, Kone, wanted only one thing, respect, which we gave to her. In return, she gave us the secret of how to kill the rhinoceros." Simbo Kalaba answered: "Yes, I know." They said: "In the village, they gave us this girl." Simbo Kalaba answered: "Yes, this is the one I have been waiting for."

Simbo Kalaba took the girl as his wife. He cared for her. The appearance of poverty washed away. Her skin shone like brass. She had children, and her children had children. And one of those grandchildren was Sundiata Keita, who in time became ruler of the country of Manding.

KENE BOURAMA, A MANDING HERO

♦ *Manding and Soninke* ♦

There was a king of the Manding people named Almami Samory. He fought wars against the Bambara and the Soninke tribes because he wanted to spread the Muslim belief in God everywhere around him. When the Europeans arrived in that part of Africa, Almami Samory fought wars against them also. Almami Samory had a brother, Kene Bourama, who fought alongside the king in all these wars.

It is told that on one occasion Almami Samory's army had been besieging the fortified town of Sikasso for many weeks. One of his wives was with him in the camp. She said to him one day: "There is something that I would like to have for my cooking—some of the leaves from that tree growing in the middle of your enemy's palace grounds." Now, for Almami Samory to get leaves from that tree he would have to take the town, and this he had not been able to do for many weeks. But he said to his wife: "If you wish it, I will see what can be done. Nothing is impossible."

Later he talked to his brother, Kene Bourama. He said: "Ah, my brother! Did you hear what my wife asked for today? She wants leaves from that tree in the middle of the town's palace grounds."

Kene Bourama replied: "My brother, that is not a problem. Put it in the hands of God. Tell your wife that tomorrow, with God's will, she will have those leaves to cook with."

Early the next morning Kene Bourama made himself ready.

He ordered his horse to be bridled. He girded himself with his waist sash. He mounted his horse. But he took no weapons in his hands, neither a gun nor a spear. He ordered his guards to stay behind in the camp, saying that he placed his trust in God to protect him.

He rode forward toward where the enemy were guarding the town. When they saw him coming, they fired their guns at him, but he was not hit. He rode through the enemy lines. They were shooting at him from all sides, but their bullets passed him by. Kene Bourama rode into the town. He rode into the palace grounds where the tree was growing and cut off a branch of leaves. He turned his horse and rode back once again through the enemy lines. Enemy soldiers were shooting at him, but their bullets did not hit him. Kene Bourama reached his own camp. He brought the leaves to Almami Samory, who gave them to his wife.

The bards made up songs about Kene Bourama's deed. The songs said that it was not mere bravery that made the deed possible, but Kene Bourama's pride and his faith in God.

Because Almami Samory's wife had said "I want leaves growing in the palace grounds of the enemy," her wish was fulfilled. And in telling this story of Kene Bourama, the songs often say:

"The wish of the woman is the wish of God."

THE HUNTER AND HIS MEDICINE SPEAR

♦ Bemba ♦

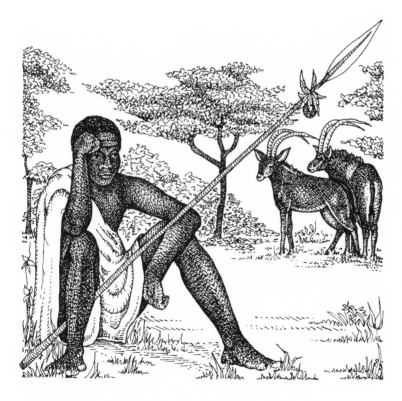

A hunter was living with his family at the edge of the bush. He spent his days at hunting. He spent his life at hunting. But though he searched in distant places he did not find much game. A bush rat now and then, an undersized antelope now and then, but he did not bring home enough meat to keep his family fed. He went to the village of his father-in-law. He said to his father-in-law: "All my days I go hunting. I search in this direction and in that direction, but the game eludes me. When I arrive at a certain place, the game has all departed from there. I go to another place and there, too, the game is gone when I arrive. I work hard to feed your daughter, but she always reproaches me, saying, 'You are lazy. Other hunters go into the bush, they come back with meat. You go into the bush, you come back with nothing.' Father of my wife, what can I do?"

The hunter's father-in-law said to him: "Yes, my son-in-law, I see that you are earnest about hunting. I myself cannot help you. But if you go to the village north of here you will find a wise old man named Sabatu. Perhaps he can do something to change your luck. Take something with you to pay him."

The hunter traded some pelts for a goat, and he took the goat with him to the village in the north. He found Sabatu sitting before his house. The man was indeed old. He was blind and his limbs were withered. The hunter sat with him and explained why he had come. "I hunt endlessly, but I cannot kill any game. It eludes me. Every day I go into the bush. I come home only with birds or bush rats. My wife berates me. She says, 'You have no ambition.' This is not living. Some evil spirit drives away anything worth eating. My father-in-law says, 'Go to Sabatu's village. He can do something for you.' Therefore I have come, bringing this goat for payment."

The old man threw cowry shells in the dust. He felt them with his fingers. He did this over and over again. At last he said: "Yes, I understand it. A bush spirit is hiding the game from you." Sabatu placed some red powder and feathers in a small cloth and tied them into a medicine packet. He said: "Attach this packet to your spear. It will overcome the bush spirit who is interfering with your hunting." The hunter accepted the packet and gave the old man the goat. Then he returned to his hut at the edge of the bush.

When he arrived there he fastened the medicine packet to the shaft of his spear. He went hunting. He did not have to go far before he saw a large antelope. He killed it and brought the meat home. Again the next day he hunted. He met another large antelope, killed it, and brought the meat home. Every day he went hunting and found game. His wife began to complain, saying, "There is too much meat. It will rot." The hunter answered: "I don't want you to say I am lazy. I will hunt. I will bring meat." He hunted. Every day he brought meat. Every day his wife complained: "The meat is rotting. The smell of it fills the air."

The hunter thought: "Every day I hunt. I never rest. Why should I work so hard? Let my medicine spear do the hunting." The next morning he sent the medicine spear out to hunt by itself. It went, and it returned bringing meat. Again the next day the hunter sent the spear out by itself. Again it returned with meat. There was more and more meat accumulating in the hunter's house. It rotted, and the air was full of the smell of decay. The hunter was stubborn, thinking that life had never been so good to him. But a time came when none of his family could stand the smell any longer. He said to his medicine spear: "Put away the hunting. It is finished." The spear was more stubborn than he. It ignored him. It went on hunting. The stench became unbearable.

So the hunter and his family took what things they could carry and moved away. They built a new house. But the wind followed them, bringing the stench of the rotting meat. Again and again they moved, farther and farther from the place where they began. Still the smell of the meat pursued them. In time they were in a distant country, and their relatives no longer knew where to find them. For a while, people said: "Where can the hunter and his family have gone?" But as the years passed, people forgot them and no longer mentioned their names.

There came to be a proverb:

"Good fortune caused the hunter to disappear in the bush."

PEKI, THE MUSICIAN

♦ *Yoruba* ♦

In a village called Orele, near the town of Otolo, there was a family with three sons named Aluge, Mokoi and Peki. Aluge, the eldest, when his time came, chose to be a farmer like his father. He cultivated the fields and grew yams and grain. Mokoi, the second son, when his time came, chose to be a trader. He went from town to town buying and selling cloth. Peki, the youngest, had not yet chosen a profession. He worked with his father in the fields sometimes, and sometimes he gathered wood for his mother's cooking fire, but often when his help was needed he could not be found. His parents worried about him, saying, "He is a strange boy. He does not do what other boys do. He would rather wander in the bush than do the work that has to be done."

Peki listened to the cries of animals and birds, and to the sound of the wind in the trees. He said to his parents: "I was in the bush today. I heard it singing." His father said: "I was in the field today, and I heard it say, 'I need hoeing.'" His mother said: "I was cooking today, and I heard the fire say, 'I am hungry, bring me wood.'"

Peki cut a small branch from a tree and made himself a flute. He wandered in the bush and imitated the sounds he heard there. From a distance, people heard Peki playing his flute and said: "The farmer farms, the blacksmith shapes iron, the trader trades, the carver carves, and Peki does nothing but play his tunes."

As Peki grew older, nothing changed. The day was approaching when he would be initiated into manhood. His father said to him: "The time is nearly here. You will be a man. You will have to choose your work." Peki answered: "It is music that I want." His father said: "Yes, but a man must do something to live. Will you farm? If so, I will help you to clear a field. Will you be a trader? If so, I will give you money to buy cloth. Will you be a blacksmith? If so, I will take you to Otolo and make arrangements for you to learn the art of forging. Will you be a weaver? I will arrange for you to learn the art of weaving."

Peki replied: "Yes, I have thought of all such things, but I want only to make music." His father was impatient with Peki. He said: "What other people do for a living, you do not want any of it. Do the yams you eat grow by themselves? No, they must be planted and cultivated. Does a hoe or a bush knife make itself? No, it must be shaped in the heat of the forge. Does cloth weave itself? No, it must be woven by human hands. You are half in this world and half in the world of unborn children from which you came. Life is work. Without work there cannot be life. Therefore you must decide what work you are going to do."

Peki answered: "Father, I want music." His father answered: "Music was here when we came, like the forest and the river. We do not have to shape it at the forge or grow it like rice. The gods gave us music. But if you persist this way the gods will become angry, and the village also will be angry because you do nothing to help it stay alive. Let me tell you, my son, what the village will say. It will say: 'Peki? Oh, he is the lazy one who grows nothing and crafts nothing.'"

Peki tried. He hoed with his father in the field, but even as he hoed, he heard music in the air and longed to play his flute. In time his father became stern. He feared that Peki would become a beggar and go from one village to another playing his flute and asking people to give him a little rice to eat. He told his son: "You will have to declare yourself. The time of your initiation is near. You have only a few days to make up your mind. If you cannot say by then how you are going to live, you will have to leave the village and begin your life as a beggar."

The day of initiation came, and Peki was initiated into manhood. His father said: "Now is the time to declare." And Peki answered: "I want only to be a musician." His father was downcast. He gave Peki a few small coins, saying, "The gods have cursed my house. You must go."

Peki left his village, carrying the only thing he owned, his flute. Feeling very sad, he went along the road toward Otolo. He put his flute to his lips and played a tune taught to him by the wind and the birds. After a while his sadness left him. He arrived at the outskirts of Otolo. He bought a little food from a vendor and sat down to eat, wondering what he would do next.

While Peki sat there, a blind singer came along the road, an old man feeling his way with a long staff. He carried an omele drum suspended from one shoulder by a leather thong, indicating that he was a singer of praise songs. The old man stopped. Although he could not see Peki, he seemed to know that he was there. He said: "Have I arrived yet at the town of Otolo?" Peki answered: "Yes, father, you are at the edge of the town." The man sat down. He said: "You also are a traveler?"

Peki answered: "Yes, I have just arrived." The man said: "You are young." Peki said: "Yes, father." The man said: "You are carrying a load of goods to the town?" Peki said: "No, father, I carry only my flute." The man said: "Ah, you too are a musician?" Peki answered: "No, father, I am not yet a musician." The man said: "Let me hear."

Peki wiped the dust from his flute and played. The man said: "Yes, you will be a musician." Then, after a pause, he said: "If you merely go here and there like I do, to one place and another, let us go together. You will hold the end of my staff and guide me." Peki answered: "Yes, I will do it." They arose. Peki took the free end of the old man's staff in his hand and walked in front. They entered the town and came to the chief's house. There the musician arranged his omele drum in front of him and began to play. People gathered. The old man sang a song of praise for the chief. He sang of the chief's generosity and good character, and about his father and grandfather. In his song he told how the chief's ancestors had come from a northern country and settled in Otolo. The chief came out of his house and joined the spectators.

While Peki listened to the singing and drumming of the old musician, he could not resist putting his flute to his lips. He began to play the rising and falling tones of the song, and whenever the musician rested his voice for a moment, Peki's flute went on, accompanying the drum. The chief was pleased with what he heard. When the singing finally came to an end, the chief brought the old man and the boy into his house and fed them and gave them money to reward them for their praise songs.

This was the beginning for Peki. He traveled on with the old man, whose name was Sholo. He learned the old man's songs. He learned to play the omele drum. The old man taught him everything he knew. A time came when the old musician died, and after that Peki traveled alone from village to village and town to town. Sometimes he stood in the center of a village singing songs the people liked to hear, after which they gave him money. Sometimes he sang praise songs for chiefs and important men. Whenever he arrived in a village, children ran to meet him, shouting, "The singing man has come! The singing man has come!"

Every year the town of Otolo celebrated the Feast of Igodo, the Yam Festival. Peki traveled from a distant place to be in Otolo on the festival day, as did many other musicians. The town was full of music and dancing. And at a certain time of the day the musicians stood before the chief's house to play for him. The chief came out and sat on his stool. One by one the bards played and sang praise songs in honor of the chief, and each of them was rewarded with money gifts. And when the singing was over, the chief called Peki to come forward, saying, "You, what is your name and where do you come from?" Peki replied: "My name is Peki, and I come from the village of Orele." The chief asked: "Where did you learn the history of my family?" Peki answered: "I learned from the old musician Sholo, who now is dead." The chief said: "Many musicians and bards have sung before my house. I have heard them all. But your singing is sweet to hear. If you will remain here in Otolo I will make you my personal singer." Peki agreed. The chief gave him a house and servants. He gave him money gifts. He gave him a special string of beads to wear, signifying that Peki was his personal musician. Peki became an important person in Otolo.

On a certain festival day when many people came to Otolo from the villages, Peki saw his two older brothers, Aluge and Mokoi, in the crowd. He went to them to talk. They did not recognize him. He said to Aluge, the farmer: "Are your crops growing well?" And Aluge replied: "The crops fail me. The rains do not come, the yams are eaten by beetles, and locusts destroy the grain." Peki said to his other brother, Mokoi: "I see by the things you carry that you are a trader. How does it go?" And Mokoi replied: "Times are bad. Everyone wants to sell, but no one can afford to buy." Peki asked: "Are your families well?" And they answered: "We survive." Peki asked: "Do you have living parents?" They said: "Yes, but they are old. For them, surviving is hard." Peki said: "Do you have brothers?" They said: "Long ago we had a brother. If he is alive now, who can tell? For he knew nothing but how to blow a flute. In time of hardship can music from a flute be eaten? He went away years ago, and we heard no more of him. Perhaps he is dead."

Peki said: "Tell your village that on the next festival day the personal drummer of the chief of Otolo will come to help the people celebrate." They answered: "Yes, we will do it."

On the next festival day Peki journeyed to Orele. He sent his servants into the village ahead of him. They beat drums and gongs and announced that the chief's musician was arriving from Otolo. A crowd gathered. Peki went first to the house of the headman, and there he sang a song of praise. Then, with

the crowd at his heels, he went before the house of his parents.
He played on his omele drum and sang:

> *In the beginning was Owner-of-the-Sky,*
> *And he created what was creatable.*
> *First he made light emerge from darkness.*
> *Then he caused the earth to emerge from the sea.*
> *He instructed his son Obatala how to make humans.*
> *He gave people iron, fire and language.*
> *He instructed Ifa in the art of divining,*
> *And Ifa passed the art on to human beings.*
> *Owner-of-the-Sky created all.*
> *Only one thing was lacking.*
> *Owner-of-the-Sky said, "Iron is great, fire is great,*
> *Yet one more thing is needed in the universe."*
> *He took a white cloud from the sky and molded it.*
> *It became a white powder in his hands.*
> *He sprinkled the powder over the earth,*
> *And it fell upon the humans he had created.*
> *Owner-of-the-Sky said, "Now I have given people music.*
> *It is my last creation, and everything is complete."*

Peki's parents were standing before their house, and now he
sang to them:

> *There were three sons.*
> *The first was a farmer, the second a trader,*
> *And the third, breathing powder from the sky,*
> *Could not do anything but play the flute.*

Therefore the third son was cast away.
He went here and there singing for cowries,
Until at last he became the chief's musician in Otolo.
Then he was honored and made a person of consequence.

Hearing these songs, Peki's parents cried. They said: "Our son Peki was sent away because of his flute, just as in the song. How he must have suffered! And now, no doubt, Peki is dead!"

Peki went to his parents and took them by the hand. He said: "No, Peki is not dead, for I am Peki." He gave them gifts that he had brought for them from Otolo, and he gave his brothers gifts also. There was a great celebration in Orele. There was feasting, drumming and dancing. And when it was over, Peki said good-bye to his family and returned to Otolo.

The people of Orele gave Peki another name. From that day onward he was called Receiver-of-the-Last-Gift-from-Owner-of-the-Sky. And they made a saying:

"Fire melts iron, but it cannot play a flute."

NGUNZA, WHO OUTWITTED DEATH

♦ *Mbundu* ♦

There were two brothers, Ngunza the elder and Maka the younger. Ngunza went on a journey to Loanda, and while he was in that place he had a dream about Maka. In the dream he heard a voice say: "Maka, your younger brother, is dead."

Ngunza returned to his village. He went to his mother, saying, "What was it that caused the death of my brother?" His mother said: "Kalunga-ngombe, he is the one. The master of Kalunga, Land of the Dead, killed him." Ngunza answered: "Then I will find Kalunga-ngombe and fight with him."

Ngunza went to a blacksmith and ordered an iron trap to be made. When the trap was finished, Ngunza took it and went to Kalunga. He put the trap in a certain place where Kalunga-ngombe was accustomed to pass, then he hid in a nearby thicket with his gun. He waited. After a while he heard a voice cry out: "I am dying! I am dying!" Ngunza came out of the thicket with his gun. He saw a person caught in the iron trap. The person said: "Do not shoot me! Come, free me from the trap!" Ngunza said: "Who are you that I should set you free?" The person answered: "I am Kalunga-ngombe, master of Kalunga, Lord of Death." Ngunza said: "So, you are Kalunga-ngombe who killed my younger brother, Maka?"

Kalunga-ngombe said to Ngunza: "I do not go out to kill people and bring them to Kalunga. The people are brought to me, that they may live on, here in this land. Your brother, I did not go searching for him." Ngunza said: "You are keeping him here in the Place of the Dead. Therefore I came to kill you." Kalunga-ngombe said: "Release me from the iron trap. Remain here for four days. On the fifth, take your brother Maka and go away with him." Ngunza said: "It is agreed." He released Kalunga-ngombe from the trap.

Ngunza remained in Kalunga. The chief of the Place of Death received Ngunza at his house. They sat together. After a while a person came by. Kalunga-ngombe asked the person: "What was it that killed you?" The person answered: "In the land of the living, on earth, I was a rich man. My wealth corrupted me. That was the cause of my dying." The person moved on. Another came, a woman, and Kalunga-ngombe asked her: "What was it that killed you?" She replied: "I was killed by vanity. I wanted a man to select me as his wife. I did everything to attract men. I did not act properly. For this reason I died and came to Kalunga." She moved on. Kalunga-ngombe said to Ngunza: "You see how it is. I do not perpetually go here and there looking for persons to kill. The tribes and villages send these persons to me." Ngunza answered: "Yes, I see how it is."

Then Kalunga-ngombe said to Ngunza: "Go over there. In a certain house you will find your brother, Maka. Take him home with you." Ngunza went to the house Kalunga-ngombe indicated. He found his brother. He exchanged greetings with him. He said: "My brother, I have come to take you back to the land of the living. Let us go." But Maka answered: "No, I do not wish to go there again. Life here is good. Here I have everything I want. In the land of the living I do not have anything. If I return with you, how will it be for me? I am satisfied here in Kalunga. I will stay."

So Ngunza prepared to return to his village. Kalunga-ngombe gave him presents to take with him to the land of the living. He gave him manioc seeds, maize seeds, pumpkin seeds, cashew seeds, okra seeds, orange seeds, and the seeds of many other plants and trees. As Ngunza departed, Kalunga-ngombe said to him: "Eight days from now I will visit you at your home." Ngunza left Kalunga and journeyed to his village. He remained there awhile. He remembered that Kalunga-ngombe was coming to visit him on the eighth day. And so, before the eighth day, Ngunza left his house and traveled toward the east. He reached the place where Ludi dia Suku lived. Ludi dia Suku was a spirit-being who had supernatural powers. Ngunza stopped there awhile.

When Kalunga-ngombe came on the eighth day, he discovered that Ngunza had left his village and gone to the east. He followed him. He came to the house of Ludi dia Suku and asked if Ngunza was there. Ludi dia Suku was eating maize. He said: "No, Ngunza was here some time ago, when we were planting our maize. Now, as you see, we are already eating our maize." (Ludi dia Suku spoke truly, for as a spirit-being he could make the maize grow fast.)

So Kalunga-ngombe went on. He came to the house of another spirit-being, also called Ludi dia Suku. Ngunza was living there, and Kalunga-ngombe said to him: "You, Ngunza, I am going to kill you now." Ngunza answered: "I did not commit any crime against you. Why do you want to kill me? You, Kalunga-ngombe, were always saying, 'I never go seeking people to kill them. Those who come to Kalunga are sent to me by the villages and the tribes.' That is what you said, but now you come looking for me just the same."

Kalunga-ngombe took his throwing-ax in his hand. He prepared to kill Ngunza. But Ngunza was under the protection of the spirit-being Ludi dia Suku. Before Kalunga-ngombe could throw his ax, Ngunza transformed himself into a Kitutu spirit. He was invisible. He was beyond the reach of Kalunga-ngombe. Kalunga-ngombe returned to the Land of the Dead without Ngunza.

This is the story that people tell about Ngunza. They call him Ngunza Kilundu, meaning Hero-Spirit, because he was a hero who defied Kalunga-ngombe and became transformed into a spirit. And every year, in one village or another, people set out food offerings in memory of his courageous deed.

TOO MUCH SEARCHING

♦ *Tswana* ♦

A man went into the bush to cut wood. As he passed along the way he looked at one tree and then another, but he did not see the one he wanted to cut. In time he came to a high rocky place, and up above he saw a good tree growing. So he climbed the hill and started to cut. But there was a rock lying where he wanted to stand. He rolled the rock away and cut the tree.

The rock that he had moved rolled downward. It bounded into a clump of bushes where a small antelope was resting. The frightened antelope leaped to its feet and ran. It ran into another clump of bushes where a buffalo was resting. Believing that it was being attacked, the startled buffalo burst out of the bushes and looked for its enemy. It saw a hunter walking nearby, and it charged at the hunter and killed him with his horns. Vultures came and hovered over the body of the hunter.

In the village, people saw the hovering vultures, and they went out to see what was there. They found the body of the hunter. They asked one another: "What caused this man to die?" They saw the hoofprints of the buffalo and asked: "What caused the buffalo to come and kill this person?" They followed the hoofprints of the buffalo and came to the clump of bushes where it had been resting. There they discovered the hoofprints of the small antelope. They said: "Ah! The buffalo was surprised by the coming of the antelope. But what caused the antelope to enter where the buffalo was lying?" They followed

71

the prints of the antelope to the first clump of bushes, saying, "Yes, here the antelope came out. But what caused him to do so?" They found the rock there, and saw the marks it had made rolling down from the high place. They said: "It is clear. A rock disturbed it. But what caused the rock to enter here where the antelope was resting?" They followed the trail of the rock and came to where the tree had been cut. They said: "Why, a man cut a tree here, and he moved the rock to do his work."

They went home. They discussed everything. They said: "When the sun rose, everything was peaceful. The land was quiet. The man went to cut wood. He passed many trees that would have been suitable. But he went to a different place and found a tree there. The trees he passed, he could have had any of them. Everything would have remained peaceful. But he went to a high place. He moved the rock. He disturbed things that were lying quietly. As a result, one thing happened, then another, and the hunter died."

So the people made a proverb:

"Too much searching disturbs things that are lying still."

FAMINE
DOES NOT MAKE
A MAN CLEVER

♦ *Zulu* ♦

A man was going on a journey from one village to another. He ate well before starting out, and he carried a large quantity of bread with him. After some time on the trail he sat down to eat. When he had eaten only a portion of his bread he found he could not eat any more. What was left of the bread he threw on the ground at the edge of the trail. It did not occur to him that he might want more bread later, or that he might meet a hungry person along the way. He thought only: "I am not hungry any more, I will leave the rest of the bread behind." He resumed his journey. Memory of the bread disappeared from his mind. In time, mice found the bread and ate it.

That was a year of plenty. Everyone had enough to eat. But the year that followed was a year of famine. The rain did not fall and the grain did not grow. Soon people were going out into the bush to search for edible roots. The man who had made the journey also went out to dig roots. What he was looking for was not easily found. He traveled a great distance in his searching, and he arrived at the trail that led from the first village to the second. Suddenly it came to his mind that this was the very same trail from which he had thrown his bread away the year before. He came to the place where he had stopped to eat.

He said: "This is the rock on which I sat! Here I stood up! Here, from this spot, I threw the bread!" He ran into the tall grass looking for the bread. He searched. He could not find it. He said: "Hau! What happened? I threw the bread here. It was this exact place." He continued searching, feeling here and there in the grass with his hands. He found nothing.

He went back to the trail and looked around him, thinking that perhaps he had made a mistake. But he said: "No, this is indeed the place where it happened! There is the anthill beside which I sat. There is the tree whose shade protected me from the sunlight. I stood here, with the bread in my hand. I moved my arm like this. I let go of the bread. It fell there in the grass." He ran once again in the direction of his moving arm. He searched again in the grass. He found nothing. He said: "I was alone. No one saw me throw the bread away. No one could have picked it up. Hau! What could have happened to it?"

The sun was setting and it was becoming dark. It was too late to go on looking for roots, so at last the man went home without anything. His family was hungry because there was nothing to eat. The next day he went hunting once more for roots. He did not look for the bread again, but he could not forget it. And one night, sitting at the fire with friends, he told them about the mystery of the bread. They laughed. They said: "Whenever did anyone see bread thrown away one year and found the next? Surely the ants or the mice have eaten it. And even if they have not, would it have been fit for a person to eat?"

The man replied: "My friends, hunger takes away a man's judgment. I thought I would surely find the bread. In my hunger it seemed to me that the bread would surely be there waiting for me, so I searched. And while I searched I forgot about digging roots. Therefore I found nothing at all to eat. Now, out of my experience, I give you a proverb:

" 'Famine does not make a man clever.' "

LIONGO,
A HERO OF SHANGA

♦ *Swahili* ♦

In the old city of Shanga there was a man called Liongo. The songs of the poets praised him as a man without fear of death. The bards called him a lion who defended what was right and avenged what was wrong. He never sought battle, but if it came to him he did not hesitate to draw his sword or place an arrow in his bow. The people of Shanga spoke his name with great respect, and persons who were unjust to others moved aside when he passed in the street. It was a time of heroes, but in Shanga, Liongo was a hero of heroes. His presence hovered over the city like a hawk in the sky.

There were some in Shanga who hated Liongo and wanted to be rid of him. They said: "Before the time of Liongo, in other times, people here were prosperous and lived without being interfered with. Traders from different countries found our city a haven of peace. If we were threatened by an enemy, we took up our weapons and drove them away. Shanga was a good city. Now we have Liongo among us, a person who came from somewhere in the gray light before dawn. He wanders through the city as if he owned it. He says, 'Such-and-such is unjust, let it come to an end.' He says, 'This merchant is a false prince, he claims what is not his,' and he drives him away. He says, 'So-and-so has been abused, let him receive justice.' We must dispose of Liongo so that he can no longer oppress and disrupt the city."

These enemies of Liongo plotted against him. Early one

morning they went in a large group to Liongo's house before he had yet put on his sword belt and his sword. They seized him and bound him with ropes. They took him to the prison and placed him there behind heavy iron doors. They said: "Now Shanga is free of this madman. The lion no longer will wander through the streets. The hawk no longer will hover above, casting its ominous shadow below."

Liongo remained for some time in the prison where they had placed him. But one night he broke loose and escaped beyond the walls of the city. Even as an outcast he did not cease being Liongo. He guarded the wells where people came for their water. He allowed persons whose character was good to draw water; those whom he deemed evil, he drove away. He guarded the roads permitting some men to pass, turning back others. Important personages of Shanga, those who had plotted against him, feared to go outside the city.

Once again they conspired to seize Liongo. They went to his camp in a large group one night and found him sleeping. Once more they bound him and brought him to the prison in Shanga. This time they fastened his wrists, his ankles, and his neck with iron fetters, and they chained his legs around a heavy post. They said: "Now this hero of heroes can no longer disturb our lives."

Liongo remained helpless in his chains and fetters. Liongo's mother sent him food every day, but the guards always took the best of it for themselves, leaving only scraps for their prisoner to eat.

The nights were long for Liongo, and he sometimes spent the dark hours singing songs. People heard his singing and liked it. If they did not hear him singing they came to the prison and called out: "Liongo, we have come to listen to your songs. Sing for us." So Liongo sang for them, composing new songs that recounted the feats of heroes and described the obligations of honorable men. Even though his heart was heavy because of his imprisonment, whenever people came and stood outside begging him to sing, he never refused. He sang:

> *What is a hero but a man who will not turn away*
> *from what he knows to be right?*
> *He will stand against wrong until his heart becomes still*
> *and his soul departs.*
> *If he hears an evil thing praised as something good,*
> *he denounces it and draws his sword.*
> *If evil seeks to hide in the dark shadows of caves,*
> *he follows and destroys it.*
> *He does not avoid death when it comes, but turns back*
> *from dying in a false cause.*
> *If his slave stands by his side when he fights a hero's*
> *fight, his slave too is a hero.*
> *If his enemy stands bravely and fights to the last,*
> *he praises his enemy as he would praise himself.*
> *But if his enemy stands before him and trembles,*
> *the hero turns away and does not judge him.*
> *The hero must forever earn merits, even if he has done*
> *great deeds. He must earn merits again and again.*

Because of his singing, Liongo was becoming more and more popular in the streets of Shanga. People everywhere were sing-

THE CREST AND THE HIDE

ing his songs. His enemies, who had sought to make him disappear from the minds of men, said to one another: "Though he lives within the walls of the prison, Liongo is a danger to the city. Therefore he must be killed." Word spread that Liongo was to die, and in time he himself heard the news.

So one day when his mother's slave girl came bringing food, Liongo ate the scraps that were left him by the guards and thanked Allah for them. The slave girl was standing outside, near a little window, and Liongo sang to her in a soft voice:

Girl, tell my mother that her son is simpleminded.
He has not yet learned the hard ways of the world.
Let Liongo's mother bake for him, and enclose in the
*   cake that which eats iron.*
In this way the hero will cut his fetters and chains.
He will be able to stand on the roofs of the city once more,
And see again the openness of the sky and green things
*   growing in the earth.*

The girl listened carefully. She went home to Liongo's mother and repeated the song. Liongo's mother understood. She went out and purchased grain and gave it to the slave girl to prepare. The girl ground the grain into flour and separated the bran from it. The mother then went out and bought files, the eaters of iron. From the bran she made a coarse cake, and baked it with the files inside. From the flour she made a delicate cake, with nothing inside. The next morning she sent the slave girl to Liongo with the two cakes. The guards took the delicate cake for themselves, and allowed Liongo to have the cake made of bran. Liongo ate the bran cake and hid the files beneath his sleeping mat.

He called out to the guards: "When shall I be killed?" And they answered: "Tomorrow." Liongo said: "Very well. Whatever Allah wishes to be done will be done. But I want to say good-bye. Ask my mother to come, and the chief and the important persons of the city, and the people of the streets. Have them gather in front of the prison. Tell them to bring horns, cymbals, and drums."

As Liongo had asked them to do, the people assembled in front of the prison. He called to them from inside, saying, "I will give you a new song. When you have heard it, sing for me. Make a loud festival sound with your voices and instruments." The people called back: "Yes, Liongo, we will do it." He gave them a song, and they took it up in the street and played their instruments. While the people sang, Liongo filed at his chains, and the sound of his filing could not be heard. When the music stopped, Liongo stopped filing and gave them another song. When they sang again, he filed again. So it went on for a long time, until he had filed the chains and fetters from his body. Then, while they were still making music, Liongo burst through the prison door and confronted the people. He grasped some of those men who had done him the greatest injury and knocked their heads together, killing them. The others fled wildly through the city. Liongo said farewell to his mother, went to his house for his weapons, and escaped once more from the city of Shanga.

He lived alone in the wilderness. He fed himself by hunting, and he cooked his food over an open fire. His enemies were afraid to leave the city; they were fearful of being caught by Liongo on the roads or at the wells. It was as if Shanga were besieged by an army.

Inside the city walls Liongo's enemies said: "It is worse now than before. How can we kill this man?" Someone suggested: "Let some young men go out and make friends with him. Let them think of a way to make Liongo defenseless for a moment, and when that moment comes they can attack him and kill him." So a group of young men went from the city and found Liongo where he was camping. They spoke to him gently. They spent time. Then they went away, and after a while they came back again. Several times they did this, and it seemed that they were Liongo's friends. One day they suggested a game. Liongo asked: "What kind of game?" They said: "Over there is a large koma tree. Let one of us climb it and throw down fruit for us to eat. After that, another man will go up and throw down the fruit. Each of us will take his turn."

Liongo was not sure that these young men were really friends. He said to himself: "I will play this game, but I will not be simpleminded." To the young men he said: "Yes, let us play the game to pass the time." So one young man went up the tree and threw down fruit, which they ate. Another man, then another climbed up and threw down fruit, until it was Liongo's turn. He said to himself: "If I climb the tree I will be helpless and they will shower me with arrows until I am dead." So instead of climbing the tree, Liongo picked up his bow. He shot an arrow into the tree and a koma fruit fell. He shot down another koma fruit. He kept on shooting until koma fruit littered the ground. The young men saw that Liongo was not going to climb the tree and become helpless. They knew that he understood their bad intentions. Fear came into them, seeing Liongo standing there with his bow in his hand and his sword hanging at his side. They turned and fled back to the city. They told the people who had sent them: "We could not do anything. Liongo is a devil."

Again those men who wanted to destroy Liongo met, asking one another, "How will we succeed in killing him?" They discussed. They argued. They could not find the answer. They agreed that someone whom Liongo would trust should go to him and find out how he might be brought to his end. They selected Liongo's nephew. They instructed him: "Go to Liongo in his camp. Because you are his nephew, he will welcome you. Discover his secret. What is the magic that will rid us of this accursed man? That is what we have to know." The nephew said: "I am of Liongo's blood. How can I do such a thing?" They answered: "Liongo is a devil. The city will not know any peace or prosperity as long as he lives. What you will do is for the benefit of all the people of Shanga. In gratitude, the city will give you all of Liongo's estate, his wealth, and his slaves."

So the nephew went out of the city and found Liongo in the wilderness where he was living. He said: "My uncle, I have come to see you." Liongo answered: "My nephew, have they persuaded you to do what you would not have done otherwise?" The nephew said: "No, my uncle, I come only to talk with you." Liongo answered sadly, saying, "I know you have come to kill me." The nephew replied: "Uncle, it is said that nothing can kill you." Liongo said: "He who is born is born to die." The nephew said: "Neither swords nor arrows have been able to kill you."

Tiredness came over Liongo, for the struggle had been a long one. He looked into his nephew's eyes. At last he said: "It was prophesied long ago that a copper needle will bring my life to an end." His nephew said: "Uncle, you are not jesting with me?" And Liongo said: "No, I am too weary, I do not jest any more."

When the nephew returned to the city he reported that only a copper needle would kill Liongo. They gave him the copper needle, and he went back to where Liongo was camped, saying, "I will stay with you awhile." Liongo knew why his nephew had returned. But they were of the same blood, and Liongo would not injure him even to defend himself. Instead, he composed a song, and through the words he spoke his feelings:

I, who am a terror to Shanga, have been kind to you.
I, who am feared by evil men, have been just to you.
I, who have been cast out of the city, have been
generous to you.
You, in your youth, understand nothing of the meaning
of life.

He sang no more, but slept. And while Liongo slept, his nephew took out the copper needle and pierced Liongo's body with it, after which he fled at once back to the safety of the city.

The pain awakened Liongo. He said: "He who is born is born to die. There is no turning back from it. My time is here." He arose. He took his weapons and went to a small knoll near the main wall of the city. He knelt there and placed his spear and his arrows on the ground beside him. He placed an arrow in his bow and aimed it toward the city. And kneeling this way, with his bow in his hand, Liongo died.

In the morning when people came to draw water from the well they saw Liongo still kneeling that way. They fled back within the city walls, crying out, "No water will be drawn today! Liongo is there guarding the well against us!" Others went out to see for themselves, and they returned saying, "It is true! Liongo kneels there with his bow in his hand!" The next day it was the same. Liongo was still there. The third day came, and nothing had changed.

The city was in distress. The people were thirsty. They went to Liongo's mother, saying to her, "Liongo is your son. He will listen to you. Speak to him. Plead with him to give us water. We are not the ones who have tried to kill him. We are the people who sing his songs in the streets."

Liongo's mother went out to the well. She saw Liongo kneeling there on the knoll. She approached him, singing a song to soothe his heart. She arrived at the knoll, and touched Liongo gently on the shoulder. When she did this, Liongo fell down and lay on the earth. Liongo's mother wept because she knew he was dead.

She went to tell the people. They came out weeping. They buried Liongo at a place called Ozi, where his tomb can still be seen. As for the young man, the nephew who killed Liongo with the copper needle, he received no reward for his unthinkable act. Instead, the people seized him and condemned him to death.

MUSA AND KOJERE

♦ Hausa ♦

In a village called Fuka there were two beggars, Musa and Kojere, who were close friends. Musa was blind, so that he could not see, and Kojere's legs were crippled, so that he could not walk, but together they were able to do what others could do. When they went out to beg, Musa the blind one carried Kojere the crippled one on his back. Kojere steered his blind partner, saying "Go this way" or "Go that way," and in this manner they went from place to place.

The two men had worked together for many years, and one was hardly ever seen without the other. In time they collected far more money than they needed. Fearing that the people of their village would come to learn of their wealth, they placed all their money in a jar and hid it in a cave, continuing all the while to dress in miserable rags.

Although they had always been like brothers, Kojere began to wish that all the hidden wealth belonged to him, and he could not get it out of his mind that he should make a plan to get Musa's share. Lying half asleep one night, the answer came to his mind. He would get rid of Musa.

The next morning when the two of them were resting alongside the road, Kojere said: "Musa, I am tired of life." And Musa answered: "I understand. Sometimes I, also, am tired of life." Kojere said: "My friend, what a load I have been on your back all these years. I am tired of being a burden." Musa answered: "Yes, you have been heavy on my back, but you have

guided me everywhere with your eyes." Kojere said: "Musa, my friend, we are part of each other. But there comes a time when men should die. Think of it. Whenever we are seen on the road, people say, 'Look, there go the miserable Kojere and Musa.' We are the lowest of all humans. Let us make an end of it. It is our time to die."

Musa answered: "If our time had come to die, why, we would be dying." Kojere said: "Musa, let us put an end to everything by throwing ourselves into the river. Think what would happen if I should die by myself. How would you get along? And if you should die before me, who would carry me from place to place? If we die together, all our sufferings will be ended." Musa answered: "Yes, it is true, but suicide is against the law of Islam." Kojere said: "Yes, I have thought of that. Yet if Allah knew of our suffering he would forgive us."

They went on discussing it until at last Musa agreed, saying, "Very well, let Allah's will be done." So Kojere crawled on Musa's back and they went to the bank of the river. Musa put Kojere down, and Kojere said: "Now, Musa, go over there to your right. A few steps will take you to the river's edge. Wait there. In a moment I will throw myself into the water. When you hear the splash, follow me. Our troubles will be over."

Musa did as he was instructed, feeling his way with his staff to the edge of the water. Kojere also moved himself closer to the water, stopping when he came to a large stone. He picked up the stone, saying "Good-bye, friend Musa," and threw the stone into the river. Musa heard the splash, saying, "Good-bye, friend Kojere." Kojere waited for Musa to jump, but Musa just stood there deep in thought. Kojere was impatient. He wanted

to call out "Jump, Musa, jump!" But he had to remain quiet because he was supposed to have died.

Musa began to speak aloud. He said: "Oh, now the friend of my life has gone and I must follow. But a man should not go quietly. He should struggle with death. *He who is about to die should struggle!* Therefore I struggle!" He swung his staff in the air. He moved here and there, striking in all directions. He struck the bushes, he struck the trees, he struck the ground, continually moving forward. "I struggle against death!" he called out again and again, all the while approaching the place where Kojere was sitting. Soon his flailing staff was falling on Kojere himself, on his shoulders, his back, and his head.

For as long as he could, Kojere kept his lips tight and did not make a sound, but finally, in pain, he cried out: "Musa! Stop! It is not death you are beating but me, your friend Kojere!" Musa did not stop. He kept hitting Kojere with his staff, calling out, "I struggle! I struggle! He who is about to die should struggle!" He went on hitting and Kojere went on crying, "Stop, stop! I am Kojere! Do not struggle any more!"

At last Musa stopped. He turned away, and with the aid of his staff he slowly found his way home. Kojere, inching along slowly, also returned home. Because of what Kojere had attempted against his lifelong friend, and because of how Musa had dealt with it, people often say when they are being abused:

"He who is about to die should struggle."

THE DEPARTURE OF THE GIANTS

♦ Mensa, Habab, Beni-Amer, Cunama ♦

Before the first Mensa, Habab, Beni-Amer, and Cunama people arrived, a tribe of giants was living in the land. It is said by some that God created the giants first, and that later he made people in the size they are today. The giants were truly giants. They used water skins made of whole elephant hides. Their spears were as tall as euphorbia trees, and the stones they threw from their slings were not pebbles but large boulders. They roasted whole cows over their fires for a single meal, and drank milk from great wooden tubs. When other tribes came into the country looking for water for their cattle and goats, the giants killed them or drove them away. Many courageous Mensa, Beni-Amer, and Habab warriors died trying to hold watering places against the giants.

Today the giants are gone, but you may still see the great stones they used for foundations of their houses, and here or there people find the remains of the enormous tombs in which the giants were buried. This story is about how the giants finally disappeared. It is told by the old people of the tribes.

God concluded that things were not peaceful because of the giants. The world was out of balance. So he sent for the chief of the giants and said to him: "It is time for your tribe to leave the world." The chief of the giants said: "Master, how have we offended you that we should have to leave?" God replied: "Your tribe has been too hard with the small people. You have forgotten that water holes were given to all the tribes for their cattle. You drive the people away, though they have done you no harm." The chief of the giants said: "Master, all tribes guard their wells. All tribes fight to protect their land. What have we done that is different?" God said: "Because you are so large and the others so small, everything is out of balance. Your tribe consumes everything. While you eat a whole cow for your dinner, the other tribes stand on a hilltop watching you swallow down enough to keep them alive for a month."

The giant chief said: "Master, it was you who created us as we are. Is the fault ours?" God said: "No, the fault is not yours, yet I have to send your tribe out of this world. Therefore I will be as kind as I can. I will give you a choice. I will let you choose how to depart. You may disappear with my curse or my blessings."

The chief of the giants said: "Who would want to receive God's curse? If we must go, send us on our way with your blessings." God answered: "Good. Let it be that way. I will lay blessings on you. Because sons are a blessing to all families, henceforth all your children to come will be sons. Because cows are a blessing on account of the calves they bear and the milk they give, henceforth all calves that are born will be females."

The chief of the giants returned to his tribe. He told the people of the blessings God had given them, and they were happy. Things came to pass as God had promised. Women gave birth only to sons, and cows gave birth only to female calves. The sons grew up. It was time for them to marry, but there were no young women to be their wives. The female calves matured, but there were no bulls for them to mate with. So in time no more children were born to the giants, and no more calves were born to the cattle. People grew old and died. Cattle grew old and died. The tribe of giants withered.

At last the chief called a council of the old people who were still alive. He said to them: "As all men can see, we are dying out from our blessings. Let us not linger here any more, waiting for the end. Let every person build a tomb for himself and cover it with a roof of stones. Let each one enter his tomb and close up the entrance. In this way we will finally depart from the world." So every person built himself a tomb and covered it with a roof of stones, after which he entered, closed up the opening, and remained there until he died. Thus the giants perished and disappeared from the face of the land.

The roofs of the tombs fell long ago, and all that remain are piles of stones. Because they remember what happened to the giants, people of the tribes sometimes say when life seems too generous to them:

"Take care, let us not die from blessings like the giants did."

ALL THINGS
ARE LINKED

♦ *Lega* ♦

There was a certain chief in a certain village. He had many slaves. Whatever he wanted to be done, he ordered it. If it was a wise thing he wanted, his various counselors said to him: "Yes, it is good." If it was not a wise thing, they said, just the same, "Yes, it is good," because if they disagreed with him he grew angry, saying, "What! Do you say the chief doesn't know what he is doing?" But the lowest of his counselors never said yes or no. If the chief asked him about a certain thing he would think for a while and then reply: "All things are linked."

It happened one time that the chief could not sleep at night because of the croaking of frogs in the marshes. Night after night he could not sleep, and he decided at last that the frogs would have to be exterminated. He told his counselors what he intended to do. One by one, as usual, they applauded him, saying, "'Yes, it is good." Only the lowest of the counselors did not speak. The chief said: "You, counselor, have you no tongue in your mouth?" The man thought for a while, then he said: "O chief, all things are linked." The chief thought: "This man knows nothing else to say."

The chief sent his slaves out to exterminate the frogs in the marsh. They killed frogs until no more frogs remained. They returned, saying, "Sir, the frogs are done with." That night the chief slept well, and he slept well for many nights thereafter. He was pleased with life.

But in the marshes, the mosquitoes began to rise in swarms because there were no frogs to eat their larvae. They came into the village. They came into the chief's house and bit him. They made his life a misery. The people of the village suffered. So the chief ordered his slaves to go out and kill mosquitoes. The slaves went out, they tried, but the mosquitoes were too numerous. They continued to plague the village. The chief called his counselors. He scolded them, saying, "When I asked you about killing the frogs, you answered, 'It is good.' Why did you not say, 'If the frogs are killed the mosquitoes will multiply'? Only one of you said something for me to think about. He said, 'All things are linked,' but I did not understand his words."

The mosquito hordes made life unlivable. People left their houses and fields and went away. They went to distant places, cleared new fields, and began living again. The old village became deserted except for the chief and his family. Finally the chief, too, took his family and went away.

Because of what happened there came to be a saying:

" 'Yes, it is good' caused a village to become deserted."

THE GREAT SNAKE
OF WAGADOU

♦ *Soninke* ♦

Before the time of the great empires of the Sudan, Mali and Ghana there was the ancient city-state of Wagadou, with its rich fields lying on all sides. Traders and caravans came to Wagadou from the north, the south, the east, and the west bringing gold and precious stones. Wagadou was also the home of brave men and heroes, whose courageous deeds are still remembered in the songs of bards. Its population was large. Because of its reputation, people came from distant places to live in this city of wealth and heroes. Wagadou was not situated near a river or lake, and it was at the edge of the broad desert, but a deep well outside its walls provided all the water it needed.

The well was the home of Bida, the great snake. In this well Bida lived, far down in its depths. It was he who made the water flow, the water that kept Wagadou alive, and whatever Bida wanted was given to him by the people. Now, one thing that Bida demanded from Wagadou was the sacrifice of a young girl each year. Some bards say that Bida ate the girl who was brought to him; some say he took the girl below and made her his wife. But when he had received his annual gift he left the well for a time and allowed the people to take the water that they needed.

One year followed another, and the time came again for a young girl to be given to the great snake at the well. The holy men of Wagadou met and discussed the matter. They decided on a certain girl. The holy men went to her family and said: "It is decided. Your daughter has been chosen."

When the girl heard that she had been chosen, she went to her fiancé, a young man named Sako, and said: "I cannot be your wife, for I am going to be given to the snake at the well." Sako became angry. He said: "No. I will not allow it. Water is life. It comes from God. It belongs to all living things. Why must Wagadou buy it from a snake? No, I will not permit Bida to have you. Go home. Say nothing to anyone. Do what they tell you to do. I will come at the right time."

The girl returned to her home. That evening the holy men took her and bound her hands and feet. There was a ceremony, with singing and dancing. When the night was darkest, halfway between one day and another, they took her to the edge of the well. They left her there and returned to the city. Sako came on his white horse and hid behind a tree, his sharpened bush knife in his hand. He waited. Time passed. Then, at last, Bida put his head out of the well. He saw the girl and moved toward her. Sako came from behind the tree. He swung his bush knife and cut off the snake's head. Instantly another head appeared where the first had been. When Sako cut off the second head, a third appeared. Sako went on fighting. He cut off the third head, then the fourth. Only after Sako cut off the seventh head did Bida die. When the snake was without any life, Sako took the girl on his horse and rode away. They did not return to Wagadou, but went to another, far distant, city.

The next day, people came to the well and saw that Bida was dead. Because it was Bida who supplied them with water, they were afraid. The well began to dry up and the rain stopped falling. A drought came to Wagadou. The once-fertile fields became parched. The grain stopped growing. Sheep and cattle died of thirst. The people suffered. For seven years no rain fell. Traders from distant places no longer came to Wagadou. When at last the storage jars became empty of water and the granaries were empty of corn, the people of Wagadou departed from their city. They began a great migration. Some went eastward toward the Niger River. Some went beyond the river into what is now Upper Volta. Some went west to Senegal. Some went south and created the Empire of Ghana.

Thus, Wagadou was abandoned by its people, and the great city died. The desert reclaimed it, and it lived thereafter only in the songs of the bards.

MOSES AND
OJJE BEN ONOGH

♦ *Somali* ♦

Once there was a man named Ojje ben Onogh. He was 4,500 years old. He was so large that wherever his shadow fell it was like night. When he went for a walk his footprints filled with water and became lakes. When he sneezed there were sandstorms, and where his clothes dragged on the ground they swept away the trees and grass, and the earth became desert. He stood in the middle of the sea to catch fish, and to cook them he held them up against the face of the sun. He planted a field of corn, and the corn grew so fast and so tall it took all the water from the earth and dried up the rivers. The people became angry, because there wasn't enough water left to grow their grain.

Moses gathered an army to fight Ojje ben Onogh. The army stretched from Hargeisa to Dahmal. It covered a valley six miles wide and six miles long. When Ojje ben Onogh saw Moses and his army coming, he picked up a mountain to throw at them. Just at this moment, a small bird flew over the mountain and dropped a tiny straw on it. That made the mountain too heavy, and Ojje ben Onogh put it down.

Moses came forward with his staff. It was thirty yards high. When he was close to Ojje ben Onogh, Moses leaped thirty yards into the air and struck him with the end of his staff. The blow landed on Ojje's ankle, and he fell dead.

Moses and his army went away. The wolves came to eat Ojje's bones. It took them forty years to eat the marrow, and they had to walk from Burao to Berbera to do it.

JOURNEY TO ASAMANDO

♦ *Ashanti* ♦

In a certain village there was a man named Kwasi Benefo. He had good fields and cattle. He and his wife were contented with life. But one day Kwasi Benefo's wife died. He grieved. He bought waist beads for her, and an amoasi, the loincloth in which women were buried. They placed her in her grave.

Kwasi could not forget his wife. Whenever he came into his house he expected to hear her voice, but there was nothing but silence. In his heart he did not feel like living any more. His brothers spoke to him, saying, "Kwasi, now you must put it from your mind. This is the way it is in the world. People die, but those who are alive must go on living. We will help you find another wife."

In a nearby village, Kwasi's brothers found a young woman for him. Arrangements were made. Kwasi married again and brought his new wife to his house. The young woman was good to Kwasi. She made life worthwhile for him once more. But before she could give Kwasi a child, his second wife also grew ill and died. Kwasi's heart hurt him. He bought her waist beads and an amoasie. They dressed her in these things and buried her. Kwasi Benefo would not be consoled. He sat in his house. He would not come out. Again, people said to him: "Kwasi, everyone dies at some time or other. Come out of the house. Mingle with your friends. Be comforted." But Kwasi felt no desire to live, and he remained in his house.

The family of the young woman who had just died heard

about Kwasi's grief. They said: "This man loved our daughter. He suffers too much. Let us give him another wife." They sent for Kwasi, and he came to their village. They said to him: "A person must grieve, but he cannot give his life to it. We have another daughter. Take her. She will make a good wife for you. You will not be alone any more. What is past is past. Let the dead live with the dead, and the living with the living."

Kwasi said: "I am grateful. But how can I take another wife when the one who died continues to speak to me when I sleep?" They answered: "Wait a while. Consider the matter." Kwasi went home and resumed working in his fields. Time passed, and at last he returned to the other village and said: "The daughter you spoke of, I have been thinking of her." They said: "Yes, she has a good character. She will make things go well in your house." They talked. They made arrangements. Kwasi married the young woman and they went to live in his house. They went on living. A male child was born to them. There was a celebration in Kwasi's village. People danced and sang, and Kwasi gave out gifts. Kwasi said: "My life is good."

One day Kwasi was working in his fields. Some women of the village came crying that a tree had fallen. Kwasi Benefo ceased his hoeing, saying: "Who cries over a fallen tree?" Then his spirit was overcome with darkness. He said: "What else do you have to tell me?" They answered: "Your wife was coming back from the river. She sat beneath the tree to rest. A forest spirit weakened the roots of the tree and it fell on her."

Kwasi went home. His wife lay on her mat. There was no life in her body. Kwasi cried out. He threw himself on the ground. He remained motionless, as if his life also had departed.

118

The people thought Kwasi Benefo too was dead. The medicine man came. He said: "No, Kwasi is not dead. He lingers between here and there." He revived Kwasi. Kwasi stood up. He made the necessary arrangements. His wife was buried in her waist beads and her amoasie. After that, Kwasi Benefo brooded. He thought: "Evil forces are working against me. Each of my three wives has died. I do not want another wife. What family would give me their daughter?" People in the village, also, were saying, "It is not good to be the wife of Kwasi Benefo."

Kwasi took his boy child and left the village. He brought the child to the family of his dead wife. After that he went out into the bush, not caring where he went. He remained in the bush, eating roots and seeds. His clothing turned to rags. He thought: "My life is wretched. I will live and die here in the bush."

One night as he lay sleepless on the hard ground, the thought came to him that he should go to Asamando, the Land of the Dead, to see the three young women who had been his wives. In the morning he went to the place in the forest called Nsamandow, where the dead were buried. He passed through it and went on. There were no paths to follow. There was no light. All was darkness. Beyond the forest he came to a place of dim light. There were no sounds in the air. No human voices, no bird songs, no calls of animals broke the stillness. Kwasi Benefo went on. He came at last to a river. He tried to ford it, but he could not do so, for the water was too deep and flowing too fast. He thought: "Here my journey comes to an end."

At this moment Kwasi saw an old woman on the opposite bank of the river. She had a brass pan at her side, and the pan was full of women's loincloths and beads. By this sign, Kwasi knew her to be Amokye, the person who welcomed to Asamando the souls of women who had died. To enter Asamando, each woman had to give Amokye her waist beads and her amoasie as payment. Amokye said to Kwasi Benefo: "Why have you come?" He answered: "I have come to see my wives who entered here. I do not want to live any longer, because death takes every woman who stays in my house. I cannot sleep. I cannot eat. There is nothing for me in the world of the living." Amokye said to him: "Oh, I have heard of you. You are Kwasi Benefo. Many persons who came through here told me about your misfortunes. But you are not a soul, you are a living person, therefore you cannot come in."

Kwasi said: "If I cannot enter, then I will stay here at the riverbank until I die and become a soul." Amokye took compassion on Kwasi. She said: "Because of your suffering I will let you come across." She caused the swift river to slow down. She caused the deep water to become shallow. Kwasi crossed from one side to the other. Amokye said: "Go in that direction. There you will find them. But you cannot see them, because they are like the air."

Kwasi went in the direction indicated by the old woman. Now he was truly in Asamando. He came to a house. He saw no persons there. He entered the house. Outside he heard the sounds of village activities. He heard people calling to one another. He heard hoeing in the fields, the clearing of brush, and grain being pounded in mortars.

Though he could see no one, a bucket of water appeared before him. Washcloths came into view. He washed the dust of the journey from his feet. He heard singing outside. He heard his three wives singing a song of welcome. The bucket and cloths disappeared, and in their place he now saw a gourd of food and a jug of water. While he ate, Kwasi heard his wives singing a song of praise. The song told of what a good husband Kwasi had been back in the land of the living. When he was through eating, the jug and gourd disappeared, and in their place was a sleeping mat. His wives invited him to rest. He lay down on the mat. His wives sang again, and in their song they told him to continue living until his natural death, when, at last, his soul would come to Asamando. When this time arrived, they would be waiting for him. Meanwhile, the song said, Kwasi Benefo should marry again, and this time his wife would not die.

Hearing these comforting words from the women he loved, Kwasi fell into a deep sleep. When at last he awoke he was no longer in Asamando, but in the forest. He arose and made his way back to the village. He told the people where he had been and what had happened. He put on fresh clothing. He began to take care of his neglected fields.

In time, Kwasi Benefo found another wife. They had children. Their home and their fields prospered. They lived on.

It is said:

"A person must grieve, but he cannot give his life to it."

CHIEF KHAMA AND
THE DUIKER

♦ *Tswana* ♦

There are many kinds of antelope in Africa, but the Tswana people feel a special kinship with the one called the duiker, because it was a duiker who saved their chief, named Khama, from death. It happened in the time of Chaka, chief of the Zulus, before anyone now living was born.

Who does not know of Chaka? It was he who united clans and tribes and created the Zulu nation. It was Chaka who sent armies out to conquer first one tribe and then another, until many people were subjects of the Zulus. Some tribes and clans fought back against the Zulu armies, but they fought in vain, and they were killed or scattered to the four winds. Others, seeing the mighty power of Chaka, laid down their spears and arrows, saying, "Great Chaka, we will not fight against you. We will be your servants in war and peace. We also will call ourselves Zulus." The conquests carried out by Chaka's armies were like boulders rolling down a steep hill. The large boulders dislodged smaller boulders, and the smaller boulders dislodged other boulders, until there was a great movement of boulders that could not be stopped. One tribe fleeing Chaka's armies drove other smaller tribes before it, and there was fighting and motion everywhere.

One of Chaka's generals was a man named Mzilikazi, of the Kumalo clan. Chaka gave him an army and sent him north to conquer more tribes for the Zulu nation. But when Mzilikazi had been fighting in the north for a while, he put his allegiance to Chaka aside and began to conquer in his own name. He thought: "Chaka is far away. It is my army that is sweeping the land clean. Therefore, what I conquer shall be Mzilikazi's." When he captured prisoners, he no longer sent them back to Chaka's camp. When he captured cattle, he kept them to feed his own soldiers.

News came to Chaka of what Mzilikazi was thinking, so he sent another Zulu army after him to subdue him and bring him home. Mzilikazi's forces were attacked. Many of his soldiers were killed. But with that part of his army that remained, he fled northward, conquering many small tribes and villages as he went. Little by little Mzilikazi's army became strong again. Though Chaka's soldiers were still behind him, in front of him the people of the villages were scattering in fear.

When Mzilikazi came to the country of the Tswana people he laid waste to the land, burning houses and the crops in the fields. The chief of the Tswanas was Khama. He gathered his warriors and said to them: "Mzilikazi is a great general. He has many soldiers. He cannot go back to Chaka, because he is an outcast among the Zulus. Therefore he will be fearless in war. We cannot hope to defeat him. Yet if we go out to fight like brave men, saying, 'This is our land, we will not give it to you,' perhaps he will turn aside and go another way."

The Tswana warriors took up their spears and shields and went out to defend their land. But Mzilikazi's army was a great force in motion. It moved against the Tswana warriors like a wide river of fighter ants and would not be turned aside. There was much slaughter, and Khama's army was scattered in many directions.

Chief Khama fled with the others. He found himself alone, pursued by a group of Mzilikazi's warriors. He was not willing to be captured and killed because if he were gone the Tswana people would have no one to lead them. When it seemed that he could not run any farther, he fell to the ground. Seeing this at a distance, Khama's pursuers chanted a song of victory. But Khama arose and ran again. He came to a dense thicket of thornbushes and plunged into it. The thorns tore into his flesh, but he paid no attention to them. Deep in the thicket he threw himself down and lay without sound or motion behind a rotting log.

As it happened, a duiker antelope, which the Tswana people call phuti, was also lying in the thicket shading himself from the sun. Though the duiker is a shy creature, he did not move from where he lay. He remained there, and Khama and the duiker lay side by side. Mzilikazi's warriors approached the thicket, shouting: "Khama entered here! Let us go in and find him!" But they were deterred by the thorns. One of them said: "Perhaps he is not here." Another shouted: "He is here! He is here in the thornbushes! We saw him enter. Where else could he have gone? There is nowhere else for him to hide." One of them said: "Perhaps he is hiding among the rocks beyond." Another answered: "No! It is here that he entered! Let us pursue him and find him!"

The shouting of the warriors frightened the duiker. He leaped to his feet and sprang from the thicket into the midst of Khama's pursuers. He bounded this way and that, dodging among them until he was in the clear, then he went racing away. Mzilikazi's men were startled. One said: "You see, it was only a duiker we saw entering the thicket!" Another said: "Nevertheless, Khama may be there also." Still another said: "No, it cannot be. If a man went into the thicket, the duiker would have come out at once. A duiker will not share a hiding place with a person. He is too timid. Khama is somewhere else." They went away. They looked in other places, but they did not find Khama.

Khama came out of the thicket. Where he went then and how he lived is not known. But in time he reappeared among his people. They were heartened, saying, "Our chief has returned!" Khama brought the scattered tribe together again.

Mzilikazi, when he had passed through Tswana country, continued his way northward. In time he reached Zimbabwe, which the whites called Rhodesia. There he stopped, saying: "This is where we will live." Mzilikazi created a new kingdom there, and the people came to be known as Amandebele.

As for the Tswana people, they were made whole again. They lived on. The story of how Khama's life was saved by the duiker is recalled by everyone. The Tswana people are indebted to the duiker, and they regard him as a totem, an ancestral relative.

NOTES ON THE STORIES

THE FIRST BARD AMONG THE SONINKE *Soninke, Mali*

Narrated by Ousmane Sako of Bamako, Mali. The story purports to account for the profession of bards, known among the Soninke as dieli and referred to by non-Africans as griots. The word dieli signifies blood as well as bard (actually, the singer of family history), thus alluding to the older brother's blood gift that saved the younger brother's life. The dieli are one of a number of castes among the Soninke, and rank above the artisan castes. Though below the grade of "nobles," in former days they had high prestige and much influence in Soninke life. This narrative was first published in *African Arts,* November 1978.

A CHIEF NAMES HIS HEIRS *Ashanti, Ghana*

Told by Kingsley Kwarteng of Bekwai-Ashanti. The story implies that in giving the head slave a field, a house, and a granary of his own, the nephew is in fact freeing him. The Ashanti tradition of nephew inheritance has been examined in numerous scholarly studies. A story purporting to explain how the tradition began, "The Coming of the Yams," appears in *The Hat-Shaking Dance and Other Ashanti Tales From Ghana,* by Harold Courlander, 1957.

THE CREST AND THE HIDE *Lega, Zaire*

Taken down in Zaire by Leo A. Verwilghen. The tale reflects on the limits of what a person may properly ask a friend to do for him. As in many other African moralizing stories, the issue is resolved by the telling of a simple tale pointing toward an applicable proverb.

THE CHIEF OF AGOGO AND THE CHIEF OF MAMPO
Ashanti, Ghana

Narrated by Alfred Kofi Prempeh. The story not only sets forth the moral responsibilities that come with power, it also comments in a proverb at the end on the social importance of being cautious about judging the words of other people.

THE WONDERFUL THING   *Bemba, Zambia*

Narrated by Oliver Kabungo. A similar tale is told among the Bene-Mukuni. See *Specimens of Bantu Folklore From Northern Rhodesia*, by J. Torrend, 1921.

KIRAMA AND KANKEJAN   *Soninke, Mali*

Narrated by Ousmane Sako of Bamako, Mali. The Sako text as recorded by the author was originally published in *African Arts*. While retaining most of the original text and its wording, the version given here is somewhat condensed, without, however, leaving out any of the narrative elements. Some of the explanations given by the narrator after the text had been set down have been incorporated into the story, conforming to Mr. Sako's wishes.

In the original version the two brothers are said to have loaded their gun with kola nuts, sheep dung, and daikai. The narrator later indicated daikai to be "a food like rice water with sour cream." For economy of language I have given the ingredients as kola nuts, sheep dung, and rice water.

KENE BOURAMA, A MANDING HERO
Manding and Soninke, Mali

Told by Ousmane Sako of Bamako, Mali. This story appears to be a fragment of a long bardic account of Almami Samory and Kene Bourama and their heroic deeds. The narrator stressed that the central feature of Kene Bourama's action was not "courage" in the usual sense but (in addition to trust in God) chivalrous pride, i.e., pride of name and reputation. Chivalry flourished in ancient times among some of the peoples of northern Africa, and there were strict codes of behavior—in particular among the "noble" classes—that had to be followed by warrior heroes. For example, a man of noble rank would not strike an enemy of a lower rank except with an object other than a sword or spear. If his enemy was of the same rank but was afraid of him, a chivalrous warrior would not strike him at all, but turn his back. Honorable behavior was more to be desired than victory, or even one's life. Kene Bourama's ride into the enemy's town without weapons, likewise, was an affair of chivalrous honor.

THE HUNTER AND HIS MEDICINE SPEAR *Bemba, Zambia*

Told by Oliver Kabungo of the Bemba tribe. A moralizing tale stressing that too much good fortune can prove to be a disaster. This "sorcerer's apprentice" theme is found in tales elsewhere in Africa. See, for example, "The Porcupine's Hoe," in *The Hat-Shaking Dance and Other Ashanti Tales From Ghana,* by Harold Courlander, 1957.

PEKI, THE MUSICIAN *Yoruba, Nigeria*

Based on a narration by Kunle Ogunleye of Mushin, Nigeria. In a general way, this tale has a theme known to many cultures—the trials and eventual spectacular success of a child held in low esteem by his family. However, the attitude of Peki's parents that music is a lowly, impractical profession is not usual in African tradition. According to the narrator of this story, in some conservative village communities, even while music was highly valued in its proper setting there was a tendency to regard a person who gave too much time to it as one who couldn't do anything else. As in comparable stories in other traditions, the parents in this instance do not reject music so much as they fear that Peki refuses to come to terms with the realities of hard living.

In the song sung by Peki about the creation of music, Owner-of-the-Sky is another name for Olorun, the supreme orisha or deity, who is also called King-of-the-Sky, Creator, Sky God and Owner-of-Endless-Space. Obatala is one of Olorun's sons, generally credited with the shaping of human beings. Ifa is known also as Orunmila, The-Sky-Knows-Who-Will-Prosper, a name which describes his role as diviner. Some of the acts of creation mentioned in the song were not performed directly by Olorun, but by lesser deities, usually described as his children. Thus, Eshu is the master linguist, and Ogun is credited with bringing knowledge of iron to the human race.

NGUNZA, WHO OUTWITTED DEATH   *Mbundu, Angola*

Properly speaking, the designation Mbundu refers to a group of peoples in Angola speaking dialects of a common language. This story, which originally appeared in *Folk Tales of Angola*, by Heli Chatelain, 1894, is identified as coming from the lower Kuanza River region. In form, substance, and spirit, the version appearing here is completely faithful to Chatelain, although language has been paraphrased freely. Some of the content has been transposed from explanations in Chatelain's footnotes.

For example, Chatelain's notes say that Suku is the name of a great spirit, and suggest that Ludi dia Suku, with whom Ngunza takes refuge, is a supernatural being. This is not developed in the actual Chatelain text, but because it seems important for an understanding of the narrative, I have written it into the present version. The closing paragraph of the story also is interpolated from Chatelain's notes.

"Ngunza, Who Outwitted Death" is another epic-like tale featuring descent into the underworld where people go after death. The Chatelain text does not explicitly say "underworld" or "under the earth," but Mbundu traditions make clear that the Place of the Dead is located there. Many stories on this theme are known among Bantu peoples and in other regions of Africa. (See, for example, the Ashanti story in this collection, "Journey to Asamando.")

One interesting aspect of this tale is the scene in which Ngunza witnesses the arrival of newly dead persons in Kalunga, and hears them explain the reasons why they died (or were killed). All the reasons point toward misbehavior on earth, and support Kalunga-ngombe's claim that people are sent to him by tribes. Nevertheless, Kalunga-ngombe goes on a long journey in pursuit of Ngunza, suggesting that he is deceitful or unreliable. But apparently there is an ambivalence in the attitudes of the Mbundu about the causes of dying. Chatelain states: "While the common people always ascribe death to Kalunga-ngombe, who wants ever more subjects for his underground kingdom, the wiser men hold that the true cause of most deaths is to be found in men's vices, crimes, and carelessness."

Although Kalunga-ngombe is represented in the story as the killer or destroyer of life, he apparently is also a spirit of fertility. This may be deduced from his act of giving Ngunza the seeds of different plants and trees to take back with him to the upper world.

For comparison with other Bantu tales of journeys to the underworld, see "King Kitamba kia Xiba" in Chatelain, *ibid.*, and *The Mwindo Epic*, by Daniel Biebuyck and Kahombo C. Mateene, 1969.

TOO MUCH SEARCHING *Tswana, South Africa*

Rephrased, from *From a Vanished German Colony, a Collection of Folklore, Folk Tales and Proverbs From South West Africa,* by Odette St. Lys, 1916. The proverb "Too much searching disturbs things that are lying still" seems to mean that it is sometimes best to leave things alone, or not to carry a thing too far, and is applicable to various social situations.

FAMINE DOES NOT MAKE A MAN CLEVER
Zulu, South Africa

This story, with restrained rephrasing, comes from *Nursery Tales, Traditions and Histories of the Zulus,* by Henry Callaway, 1868. The substance and spirit of the original remain intact. Africans perceive dangers in all extreme situations. There are proverbs and tales observing that unwise or silly actions can result from too much good fortune as well as bad fortune. See, for example, "The Hunter and His Medicine Spear" in this collection.

LIONGO, A HERO OF SHANGA *Swahili, Tanzania*

This epic narrative is taken from *Swahili Tales as Told by Natives of Zanzibar,* by Edward Steere, 1870. Steere's prose has been freely rewritten in the present version, which has also drawn on the "Poem of Liongo," written in archaic Swahili by the poet Sheikh Abdallah Muyuweni, for supportive passages and sentiments. As given here, however, the narrative follows Steere's version in plot, incidents, descriptions, and denouement, and remains faithful to the events as he set them down. For those who do not have access to the Steere book, both the story and the poem are to be found in *A Treasury of African Folklore,* by Harold Courlander, 1975.

The oral literature of the Swahili is a blend of Bantu, Indian, and Islamic traditions, and in its chivalric aspects it has ties with the heroic literature of other parts of North Africa. The precise period of Liongo's life is not generally known, but the facts as given in the story are deemed to be true, and his memory is revered.

MUSA AND KOJERE   *Hausa, northern Nigeria*

Recounted by Ezekiel Aderogba Adetunji, a Yoruba of Ilesha, as told to him by a Hausa friend.

THE DEPARTURE OF THE GIANTS
Mensa, Habab, Beni-Amer, Cunama, northern Ethiopia and Sudan

This story is based on notes taken by the author in Eritrea, and on variants told in *Storia de Mensa*, by K. G. Rodén, 1912, and in *Publications of the Princeton Expedition to Ethiopia*, by Enno Littmann, 1912. All three sources are essentially similar, differing only in minor details. The Littmann and Rodén versions come exclusively from the Mensa, but the tradition of the end of the giants is known to neighboring Cushitic and Nilotic peoples as well as to the Amhara-related Habisha of Eritrea. The tale is a legend accounting for the "giants' tombs" that are sometimes encountered, and likewise for the fact that giants no longer exist. It also points the moral that what might seem to be a blessing could in fact be a curse, a theme that turns up elsewhere in African oral literature. See, for example, the story (and notes for) "The Hunter and His Medicine Spear" in this collection. The tradition of a race or tribe of giants is mentioned in the Old Testament. See the story "Moses and Ojje ben Onogh" and its explanatory notes, also in this volume.

135

ALL THINGS ARE LINKED   *Lega, Zaire*

Taken down in Zaire by Leo A. Verwilghen. The story belongs to a group of moralizing tales demonstrating that a foolish action can jeopardize an entire community. This preachment is common to many African cultures, and it is implicit in another tale in this collection, "The Hunter and His Medicine Spear." "All Things Are Linked" also comments on the fallibility of chiefs, whose whimsical decisions may cause an entire village to suffer. Social comment is implicit in the unwillingness of the chief's advisors to say plainly that his proposals are not good.

THE GREAT SNAKE OF WAGADOU   *Soninke, Mali*

Narrated by Ousmane Sako of Bamako, Mali. The legend is a brief version of a long epic having to do with the heroes of Wagadou. A longer version is to be found under the title "The Fight With the Bida Dragon" in *African Genesis*, by Leo Frobenius and Douglas Fox, 1937. In the longer version, it is not Sako who kills the dragon or snake, but another hero, Mamadi Sefe Dekote. Sako is sent out to kill Mamadi Sefe Dekote for what he has done, instead of which Sako purposely allows him to escape. In its longer form, the story of the Bida monster is still sung by Soninke dieli, or bards. As given here, this narrative was first published in *African Arts*, November 1978.

MOSES AND OJJE BEN ONOGH   *Somali, Somalia and Ethiopia*

Told to the author by Mosa Mohammed, and reprinted here from *The Fire on the Mountain*, by Harold Courlander and Wolf Leslau, © 1950, 1978. The tradition that giants once lived in this region appears to be of considerable antiquity, and is referred to in the

Old Testament. During the Israelites' journey from Egypt, they encounter a tribe of giants known as sons of Anak (Numbers, 13). They avoid confrontation with these giants, but come in time to Bashan, whose ruler is a giant named Og (Numbers, 21). The tale given here, an Islamic elaboration of Old Testament descriptions, encapsulates the battle that ensues, with Moses and Ojje ben Onogh (i.e., Og, son of Anak) fighting as champions of their respective tribes. This Somali version comes to us through the oral tradition, but the story also is found in written form, appearing, for example, in a fourteenth-century Persian manuscript, *Jami' at-Tavarikh,* with an illustration of the epic battle. The hyperbolic elements in the Somali variant suggest a series of improvisations by oral narrators.

JOURNEY TO ASAMANDO *Ashanti, Ghana*

Told by Kingsley Kwarteng, of Bekwai-Ashanti. Though the narrator did not describe it as such, Asamando, the Land of the Dead, is in the underworld. In a longer variant, Kwasi Benefo loses eight wives before he makes his underworld journey. For another tale about a journey to the underworld, see "Ngunza, Who Outwitted Death," elsewhere in this collection.

CHIEF KHAMA AND THE DUIKER *Tswana, South Africa*

The story of the pursuit of Khama by enemy warriors was set down by Daniel Marolen, a Shangaan (or Tsonga) of South Africa. The introductory portion of the story, explaining the identity of Mzilikazi and the circumstances of his attack against the Betswana, is taken from historical sources.